Strengthening Your Walk:
A Daily Devotional

GET STRONG ANTHOLOGIES
Dig into the Word!

Strengthening Your Walk:
A Daily Devotional

Brought to you by:
Revolutionary Disciples Media
Compiled by
Ayani_Meli and
Angela C. Washington

GET STRONG ANTHOLOGIES
Dig into the Word!

Copyright © 2015 by Revolutionary Disciples Media

ISBN: Softcover 978-1-941574-00-3

All rights reserved. No part of this book may be reproduced or transmitted in any form or by any means, electronic or mechanical, including photocopying, recording, or by any information storage and retrieval system, without permission in writing from the publisher or copyright owner. Unless otherwise indicated, Scripture quotations are taken from the King James Version of the Bible. This book was printed in the United States of America.

Cover: JWGraphics

To order additional copies of this book, contact: Your favorite author or

Revolutionary Disciples Media
PO Box 32 Sylvania, GA 30467

Phone: 774-7REVDIS

www.revolutionarydisciples.com
www.getstronganthologies.com
revolutionarydisciplesmedia@gmail.com

Book ID: Strengthening

Disclaimer: We have endeavored to write what we believe to be in line with God's written Word. The Holy Bible is THE book that contains the inerrant Word of God. Most scriptures are of the New King James Version, unless otherwise specified; however, a few are from the New International Version.

Preface

This devotional was divinely inspired. A couple of years ago, He laid it on our hearts to do a single devotional. Life happened; but delay was not denial. In His own timing, He provided the format, and directed us toward the specific contributors. This is His Work. He speaks throughout the volume! As such, you will notice recurrent themes about love, faith, strength and obedience, just to name a few.

This unique concept of having a different author for each month led to this compilation of Holy Spirit inspired devotionals, by fourteen different Men and Women of God. Each has their own style and matchless life experience. We as humans all walk different paths to reach the same destination. We endeavor to make that path a little easier to traverse; thereby making your walk a little more stress free. There is room on specific devotionals for you to make notes or lists, so that as you return and peruse those notes, you can see your progress toward your spiritual goals.

Abbas Word is living and fluid. It provides milk for the babes and meat, rich in nutrients, for those ready for solid food. We endeavored to offer something for every reader within the pages of this book. You may laugh, you may cry; all in all, you will examine yourself, your life, the circumstances in which you find yourself involved and ultimately, your walk with Christ. There is strength in these pages. Get Strong!

Acknowledgments

We would like to express gratitude to the many people who caught the vision for this Get Strong Anthology series; to all those who provided support or offered comments, advice, read, wrote, and assisted in the editing, proofreading and design. God bless you!

To name a few individually, we would like to pay special tribute, warmth and appreciation to the persons below who made this devotional project successful and assisted us to reach our goal:

The contributors, your words and wisdom will live on in perpetuity.

Mrs. Melvina Pratt-Harris, thanks for your hard work.

Dr. Mark H. Stevens, your input was invaluable.

Last but not least; those who lent emotional support deserve mention as well:

Dr. Lafils Rivers, your support and prayers are always welcome and appreciated.

Our families, thank you for your sacrifices.

Table of Contents

Introduction

Have you ever found yourself out of sorts during the day? Are you unhappy? Do you need help overcoming trials and tribulations and believe that no one else has ever had these experiences? There is hope! Common sense tells us that some problems can be solved by restructuring your time, making wiser choices and working harder. That may be true at different times, but in some cases, it could be a soul issue.

Not one person on this planet has it ALL together. We want to help you unclutter your spirit and reach that very intimate relationship with God that your soul desires. If you want to make changes, start with your prayer life. If you do not have time to praise and worship God, make time. Some of the devotionals will shepherd you into a place of worship; while others will bring unique and new revelations.

These are awesome and anointed men and women of God! They all have a voice, and they speak loudly. We wanted this book to be personable and touch you right where you live. The devotionals are written in their voice, from their viewpoint and from their life experiences and Godly wisdom. As such, each author wrote what they received from the Heart of God.

The chapters are laid out in an easy to read format. The scripture for the day is provided for you; but you are encouraged to have your bible handy to read the entire chapter, if necessary. No specific year has been targeted for this work, as it is to be read from year to year, as long as you need encouragement.

We pray that each day brings before you exactly what God has ordained for that day. There are prayers, anecdotes, jokes and wisdom, all within the pages of this book. We also invite you, if you have not done so, to start a journal in conjunction with this devotional. If you need to work your way up to journaling, use the space inside the devotional to write what God has revealed to you or laid on your heart.

Each time you pick up this devotional, you may be surprised, edified or intrigued by what He is saying. Open your mind to the things of God and open your spirit (spiritual ear) to hear his voice!

Notable Inspirational Prayers

To be a Christian without prayer is no more possible than to be alive without breathing.   ~~Martin Luther King, Jr.

March

By: Phyllis Smart

Day 1

Purpose

3 knowing that the testing of your faith produces patience.
James 1:3

Have you ever asked yourself why do we as Christians go through so many trials? One thing to consider is that satan only attacks Believers. Why would he waste his time on people who follow him? Could it also be that God is developing character in you. Nothing that we go through is wasted material for God, God uses our mistakes and mishaps to help us grow. He uses every trial to direct us in His ways, if we are willing and obedient. When you operate on Faith and authority satan cannot continue his work of discord, hatred or confusion in your life. Jesus dying on the cross made the provision for Us. God's ultimate desire for us is to live life in our purpose.

What is your purpose? If you are unsure, have you asked God to reveal it to you?

_____
_____
_____
_____
_____
_____
_____
_____
_____
_____
_____
_____
_____

⌐Day 2⌐⌐

We Are Forgiven

**9 To the Lord our God belong mercy and forgiveness, though
we have rebelled against Him.
Daniel 9:9**

Do you allow the failures of your past to haunt you? I can
remember many times that I truly walked in fear of people
finding out about things that I knew I had done. Fear kept a
strong grip on me for a very long time. Satan the accuser of the
brethren continuously reminds us of all the mistakes that we
have made in life. If that is you, right now where you stand,
rebuke Him with the truth that Christ died so that we may be
FREE. Stop listening to the lies of the enemy. Instead turn to the
Word of God and confess what He says about you. There are
many in the bible that God used and they had made numerous
mistakes. Saul who became Paul persecuted Christians. (1
Timothy 1:15) Once converted he did not sit in his past and
wallow over what he had done but he accepted what God said
about him and stood on the Word of God. Put the Past behind
you and walk in the Truth of God.

⌐Day 3⌐⌐

We All Sin

**20 For there is not a just man on earth
who does good And does not sin.
Ecclesiastes 7:20**

We all have sinned and fallen short. When was the last time you
had to ask God for forgiveness—an hour Ago, yesterday or last

week? We all live with sin every day of our lives. We see it on TV, in movies, in our children, in our spouses, co-workers, and friends. Sin is usually easy to spot in others but when it comes to us we forget about that PLANK in our very own eye. It is very easy to be blinded to our own sins. Right now ask the Holy spirit to show you things that you have done wrong. Confess these things to God and ask for forgiveness. Forgiveness can only come through the Blood of His son Jesus.

Lord help me with:

_____

_____

_____

_____

_____

Day 4

Hope is Alive

35 for I was hungry and you gave Me food; I was thirsty and you gave Me drink; I was a stranger and you took Me in; 36 I was naked and you clothed Me; I was sick and you visited Me; I was in prison and you came to Me.
Matthew 25:35-36

We are living in a time where many people are displaced. Either they have been laid off, can't find a Job or lack the education needed to get a good job. This has propelled millions of families into poverty and despair. I wonder what has happened to the love of Christ for others. We walk by and see many in bad situations and we refuse to help or offer assistance. I command you to pray without ceasing for the hungry and the needy. Pray for those that are behind prison walls with no hope. Do what you are able to do, so that they may live and know the Love of the Father. Let them see the Love of Christ through you.

⟶ Day 5 ⟶

Speaking Life

13 You shall not murder.
Exodus 20:13

Do you pat yourself on the back because you strive to obey the ten commandments? You most likely stick to the letter of the Word, but what about the Spirit of the Word? Most people when they see or hear the word MURDER they state strongly that they would never do that or they would never think about murdering someone. Be very Careful!!! Jesus teaches us in Matthew 5:21-22 that unjust anger and refusing to forgive are acts of murder that we commit in our hearts. He says, "Do not murder, and anyone who murders will be subject to the judgment." Now ask yourself how often have you killed one another by holding grudges, hatred and anger over them? How often have you worked to secretly tear down others with your words and speaking death over their lives and their works? I challenge you today to search your heart for signs that you are holding grudges or failing to forgive. I challenge you to ask God to forgive you and to help you speak life instead of death. The Murdering MUST STOP now.

⟶ Day 6 ⟶

Back To The Basics!

15 You shall not steal.
Exodus 20:15

We are taught as youngsters to obey and live by the ten commandments. Now we as Christians have a tendency to look over this commandment. We think that if we are not shoplifting, robbing a bank or carjacking this does not apply to us. Well let me help you. If you are bringing office supplies home, riding the time clock at work or not tithing these are all forms of theft. We should be thankful to God for everything that He has given us. We need to trust Him for the things that we do not have. Rather than stealing decide that you will be a giver. God blesses those that give. It is truly better to give than to receive.

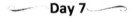 Day 7

Hitmen

16 You shall not bear false witness against your neighbor.
Exodus 20:16

This is one more commandment we tend not to obey; many are guilty of this. When engaging in a conversation with a person face to face, we may be uplifting and speaking life into them; however, behind their backs we are tearing them down. God has instructed us not to be a member of the "Character Assassination Police." CAPS are like hired assassins.

Much damage can be inflicted by such a small part of the body (James 3:3-6). Lies destroy careers, churches, families, marriages and reputations. Avoid words that inflict pain. Speak words will help edify and uplift someone's spirit. Our emotions can propel us into a whirlwind of negativity, that just continues to spin out of control. Today steer clear of gossip and speak truth.

Day 8

Not Ashamed

33 But whoever denies Me before men, him I will also deny
before My Father who is in heaven.
Matthew 10:33

Many have told me that they have seen folks who were supposed to be followers of Christ in compromising situations. Which mean they were not acting as if God was in their lives. We as believers have a tendency to be ashamed to show our holiness to the world. We are called to be witnesses for God. Christ paid a price we could not afford to pay, so when we have a chance to witness or be a witness for Christ then we need to do so. You do not have to beat people over the head with a bible either. All you need to do is be willing and ready, at all times, to share the good news.

Day 9

Empty Yourself

11 You will show me the path of life; In Your
presence is fullness of joy; At Your right hand
are pleasures forevermore.
Psalm 16:11

Fill me Up God, till I overflow, I wanna run over... I Love this song it ministers to me daily. God allowed me to know that He can meet me at the point of my deepest need. In His presence, He has everything that I need to manifest His anointing and my breakthrough. You must get to a place physically, emotionally, and spiritually where you want nothing but God. You want His anointing on your life and will settle for nothing less than His presence. Before God can do this, we must empty ourselves of everything. We must pour out our dreams, our hopes and our plans so that He can pour His anointing into us. God is saying give me what you have and I will give you what I have and what you need. The anointing of God turns the natural into the supernatural.

Peaceful Thaddeus Miles Photography

Day 10

Do You Really Want God?

4 Delight yourself also in the Lord, And He shall give you the desires of your heart.
Psalm 37:4

I can remember in my early walk with God, I wanted Him so desperately but I still could not let go of some of the things that were holding me captive to the world. One day my grandmother told me, "you cannot have one foot in the church and the other in the world." She said, "God sits high and looks low." At that point I knew that I had to become sold out for God. From that day on, it became my ultimate goal for Him to be pleased with my life. I ask you, do you desire God? Do you seek Him daily? Do you commune with Him often? Do you meditate on His word? Do you listen to Him speak? The proof of your desire for Him is how you pursue Him. As Christians, we should seek Him daily, continually and diligently; as we do, we should delight in Him. Then God will give us the desires of our hearts.

Day 11

Waiting on the Promise

31 But those who wait on the Lord Shall renew their strength; They shall mount up with wings like eagles, They shall run and not be weary, They shall walk and not faint.

Isaiah 40:31

Waiting, for me, is one of the hardest things to do. Since we live in a microwave generation, we always want things fast. If you practice patience and learn the posture of waiting, the process can go quickly and the transition quite smoothly. God has promised us some things and He is not on our timetable. God wants to fill us with His spirit, so we can fulfill His purpose for our lives. When the promise of the Holy Spirit came down in the form of a mighty rushing wind and tongues of fire, He changed a group of fearful believers into bold disciples. They changed the world with the good news of Christ. Wait Upon Him and you will taste and see the goodness of God in your life.

My prayer today: *Lord I wait patiently on the things you have for me, in Jesus' name, Amen.*

Day 12

All Things New

17 Therefore, if anyone is in Christ, he is a new
creation; old things have passed away; behold,
all things have become new.
2 Corinthians 5:17

When you decide to accept Christ as your Lord and Savior, you become a new creature, feel like a new person, and you act differently. You speak differently and your thoughts are now Godly thoughts. You have professed that you have left your old self behind and are embracing the new. You are professing that you have put off your old self and that you desire to become one with Christ. When you become one with Christ, we need to examine what we are doing at all times. Don't hang onto the desires of the flesh. This can cause unnecessary problems. Walk with those who walk with Christ. This will help to strengthen you as you begin this journey. You have to throw off all of your old ways and embrace who Christ has made you to BE.

Day 13

Freedom

3 Remember the prisoners as if chained with
them--those who are mistreated--since
you yourselves are in the body also.
Hebrew 13:3

I have never been to prison but I have known people that have. They say that it is not an experience that they would want anyone to endure. I may not have been in a physical prison but

I can recall many times where I have been in a mental and emotional one. To be bound in your thoughts and emotions, feels like a life sentence. "Life in A Cage" is what I frequently called my situation. Jesus' Blood set many of us free but there are many who are still bound. When I observe someone going through, I have compassion because I understand fully what it is to be bound. There are so many that are still spiritually bound. Jesus paid the price for us to be able to live in eternal Freedom. Romans 6:18 says, *you have been set Free from all sin.*

Day 14

Unyoked

27 It shall come to pass in that day That his burden will be taken away from your shoulder, And his yoke from your neck, And the yoke will be destroyed because of the anointing oil.
Isaiah 10:27

The anointing is God's supernatural power to destroy every yoke, every bondage in any and every area of your life. Be it physically, financially or spiritually. The anointing opens blind eyes and puts homes back together. The anointing of God destroys every yoke. We have to realize that the day will come when we have to surrender to God's anointing; we cannot do this on our own. God has to become the center of our life. God and God alone has the power to set us free. You must realize that there is nothing too difficult for God. No yoke of any kind can withstand the power and presence of God. Freedom is here just receive it and trust God.

What yokes need to be broken in your life?

_____

_____

_____

_____

_____

— Day 15 —

Not An Option

23 Now may the God of peace Himself sanctify you completely; and may your whole spirit, soul, and body be preserved blameless at the coming of our Lord Jesus Christ.
1 Thessalonians 5:23

We are called to be holy and sanctified, as believers. Preachers like Oral Roberts understand that holiness is not an option but a lifestyle. He lived his life in a humble and dedicated way to God. These men served God and worked tirelessly and prayed without ceasing. Today many churches or ministries have neglected teaching on self-control, discipline and holiness. One component cannot operate without the other. *Be Holy because I am Holy*, states Leviticus 19:2. That is saying that our daily lifestyle should reflect our daily communication with God. We should do this through fasting prayer and service. Holiness is tight but it will always be right.

— Day 16 —

Living in Peace

16 For God so loved the world that He gave His only begotten Son, that whoever believes in Him

should not perish but have everlasting life.
John 3:16

There is balance in life, when we live in peace; God has purposed for us to live this way. There are many things that come to try and upset our peace. Death, divorce and loss of jobs are just a few setbacks that come to take our peace. During these times is when we need to draw closer to the Father. Life happens to us all but the important thing is how we handle life when we are faced with challenges; when all we can do is stand on His Word. When the storms blow, know that you are anchored in Christ. He did not bring you this far to allow life to pull you down. Know that there are others that have come before you and many to come after; they will also have storms. But know that on Christ, the solid rock, you stand and all other ground is sinking sand.

Day 17

Giving

2 that in a great trial of affliction the abundance of their joy and their deep poverty abounded in the riches of their liberality. 3 For I bear witness that according to their ability, yes, and beyond their ability, they were freely willing,
2 Corinthians 8:2-3

One of the best times to show the world that we serve a mighty a God is during a financial crisis. Then It is evident Who is able to do greatly and abundantly over what we can ask or think. It truly gives "I AM" the opportunity to brag on us, to say to the enemy "That's my child, the one that will trust me even when they don't see it." We must show the devil we do not depend on the world's economic system but the economic system of heaven. We have to begin to give out of our need. Will we trust Him for the impossible? He will never allow the devil to outdo Him in anything. So know that if there is a need, God is well and able to provide for His people. Trust that God will provide out of the heavenly economy not the world's.

⌒⌒⌒ Day 18 ⌒⌒ ➣

Growing Up

11 Now no chastening seems to be joyful for the
present, but painful; nevertheless, afterward it
yields the peaceable fruit of righteousness
to those who have been trained by it.
Hebrews 12:11

God accepts us where we are and loves us too much to leave us. Growing can be painful but He wants to help us be the best we can be. For me, growing up was scary. I wanted to remain Daddy's little girl. Father God, wants to refine us, removing all impurities. The Bible is full of people that He had to refine. Paul endured trials for the sake of the Gospel but millions may have been saved because of his letters. Quitting should never be an option; our mandate is to endure. Are you willing to stay in the battle knowing God has your back? Mighty vessels of God are built in battles, forged in the fires of opposition and finished on the Potter's wheel. This all shows God's unfailing Love for us.

⌒⌒⌒ Day 19 ⌒⌒ ➣

Endurance

8 You are already full! You are already rich! You have reigned
as kings without us--and indeed I could wish
you did reign, that we also might reign with you! 9 For

I think that God has displayed us, the apostles, last, as men condemned to death; for we have been made a spectacle to the world, both to angels and to men. 10 We are fools for Christ's sake, but you are wise in Christ! We are weak, but you are strong! You are distinguished, but we are dishonored!
Corinthians 4:8-10

The devil attacks at every place of weakness, hoping to discourage us. He is praying that we will compromise, stumble and fall. When we begin to grow, satan tries to discourage us from what God says about us. His purpose is to come and sift us like wheat. This can only happen if we allow our focus to be shifted from God's way, to the way of the enemy. That is why it is so important to keep your eyes on the things of God. The enemy believes that this will cause the believers to be destroyed. We have to know that the testing will come and we must be steadfast in the Word of God. We are to meditate day and night. When you resist the devil your faith will begin to grow. You must have a committed heart to God. You must also know that the enemy has no power! We already have the victory; know that this will keep us though the hard times.

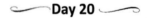Day 20

New Wine

17 Nor do they put new wine into old wineskins, or else the wineskins break, the wine is spilled, and the wineskins are ruined. But they put new wine into new wineskins, and both are preserved.
Matthew 9:17

This passage of scripture speaks volumes because many times we try to use the same old things; attempting to put it a new form. What is old should stay with what's old and what's new should stay with what's new. You have to allow the Father to shape you from the old into something new. I have been told that it is insanity to do the same thing over and over again, expecting a different result each time. The wineskin represents us. Are we willing to be shaped as God desires to shape us or do we desire to stay in the old skin where the skin is harder to bend or mold? There are times when we are going to have to be required to get on the Potter's wheel. So allow Him to shape you. He will not work with you unless you allow Him. It takes faith and His help to shed the old man and to allow Him to shape you into a vessel that can be used.

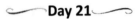**Day 21**

Keep Watch

> 74 Then he began to curse and swear, saying, "I do not know the Man!" Immediately a rooster crowed. 75 And Peter remembered the word of Jesus who had said to him, "Before the rooster crows, you will deny Me three times." So he went out and wept bitterly.
> **Matthew 26:74-75**

Many times in my life, I have been thrown under the bus. I felt betrayed and used by some of the closest people to me. When that happens, if you are not strong you may be deeply wounded to the core. Every since the fall of man, the enemy has been actively working to sow doubt and denial. The enemy's job is to be a seducer. He seduces many to step out of character. You see the enemy sees the anointing on your life and it is his desire to destroy that. The enemy tries to instill fear and doubt in whatever way he can. Do not give the enemy the opportunity to sow seeds.

Day 22

Ah! The Humanity!

14 And the grace of our Lord was exceedingly abundant, with faith and love which are in Christ Jesus.
1 Timothy 1:14

No one can keep the law perfectly. We must realize that we are human and we will make mistakes. During the old testament they had to make atonement for their sins. Since the death of Christ we no longer have to make atonement for our sins or be subjected to the law. Jesus came so that we should be clean and washed of our sins. This does not exempt us from not sinning but it allows us to know that we are able to come back to the Father. So if you have sinned, don't beat yourself up too badly because we all make mistakes. The gift of grace is there with no strings attached and we can do nothing to earn it. It is freely given to those who believe.

Day 23

Our Mission

24 But none of these things move me; nor do I count my life dear to myself, so that I may finish my race with joy, and the ministry which I received from the Lord Jesus, to testify to the gospel of the grace of God.
Acts 20:24

We all have been given a mission from the Lord; every minute that we are on Earth should not be wasted. We have been called by God to be witnesses of His grace. Romans 5:8 states, *God demonstrates his love for us in this, while we were still sinners, Christ died for us.* We have to receive the calling on our lives that God has given us. It is our mandate to win souls. It is our mission to share the good news with all. Jesus commanded every believer to Evangelize (Matthew 28). So it is our duty to be in the highways and the byways witnessing for Christ. <u>Know that we are all here for purpose.</u>

——— Day 24 ———

Be Separated

17 Therefore "Come out from among them And be separate, says the Lord. Do not touch what is unclean, And I will receive you." 18 "I will be a Father to you, And you shall be My sons and daughters, Says the Lord Almighty."
2 Corinthians 6:17-18

What do you value more than God? Do you have idols in your tent—things that you value more than God? Idols may include: your need to be right, your job, your children or your spouse. Things that occupy God's space are idols. The Lord tells us plainly in Exodus 20:4-5, that He is a jealous God and instructs us not to make graven images of anything. The Blood of Jesus can break every bondage. We must separate ourselves from that which is not of God. We must get the ungodly things out of our lives and seek to have a right relationship with God.

——— Day 25 ———

Are You Rooted In Self?

25 For what profit is it to a man if he gains the whole world, and is himself destroyed or lost?
Luke 9:25

Wrong or selfish motives will not please God. We can fool man who looks on the outward appearance but we cannot fool God. When you find individuals that must always be the center of attention or the leader in everything, those are definitely self-centered individuals. The only way to be in the Will of God and to have the mind of God is through having a deep and abiding relationship with Him.

Our motives should be to please God not ourselves; we were created to be a pleasure to God not to ourselves. *You are worthy, O Lord, To receive glory and honor and power; For You created all things, And by Your will they exist and were created.* (Revelation 4:11) God is pleased with us when our motives are selfless, instead of selfish.

⌒ Day 26

Destined for Greatness

10 For we are His workmanship, created in Christ Jesus for good works, which God prepared beforehand that we should walk in them.
Ephesian 2:10

Many of us are accustomed to settling for less than God's best. Many times we feel that we are not worthy of the blessings He wants to give us. There is much greatness that can be found in the things of God. The greater one lives in us and He has made us higher than anything. I have heard many say that they have mansions and riches in Heaven. God promises a better life here on Earth and I want all of mine here! You have to believe that God has a greater purpose for us. You <u>must</u> believe all the promises of God.

What has God promised you?

_____

_____

_____

_____

_____

Day 27

Never The Same

3 Therefore the showers have been withheld, And there has been no latter rain. You have had a harlot's forehead; You refuse to be ashamed.
Jeremiah 3:3-3

We are living in a moment in time when God is moving in an extraordinary manner concerning His people. God is moving into the ordinary with extraordinary demonstration of His character. These are some of the final moments in history. There is a brand new day on the horizon.

In this hour, God is doing a quick work. God is about to take His people to another level. The next time you call on the name of God, be ready to gain new ideas and new concepts. All you have to do is seek the Lord while He can be found. Allow God to direct your life and allow Him to fulfill His divine purpose. Know that you are never alone; God is changing your life supernaturally.

Dear God,
if today I lose my hope,
please remind
me that your
plans are better
than my dreams.

Day 28

The Harvest

2 Then He said to them, "The harvest truly is great, but the laborers are few; therefore pray the Lord of the harvest to send out laborers into His harvest.
Luke 10:2

There are millions of souls that are saved yearly but there are millions of people who don't hear the gospel consistently. They have no idea about the saving grace of Jesus. God has given US the task of Evangelism. We have a very big job to do but an even bigger God to help us do it.

I see many young people daily walking the streets and drinking and I say, "where are the witnesses?" The church needs to rise up and reach out. We need to let go of pride and our desire to remain in what's familiar. Jesus called us to make disciples of all nations. We must find more workers to reap a great harvest of souls for the Lord.

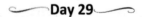Day 29

Open Your Mouth

10 I am the Lord your God, Who brought you out of the land of Egypt; Open your mouth wide, and I will fill it.
Psalm 81:10

God wants to fill our mouth with His words daily. Many times we swallow whatever the devil throws our way. We can put a stop to this by just allowing the Word of God to fill us. We need to testify about the goodness of Jesus and all He's done. Find

three people and tell them about the goodness of the Lord. Don't waste time or thoughts worrying about what the world thinks about you. God is the ruler of everything and He loves you.

You can open your mouth with prayer and praise. Choose your words wisely because you want to speak life not death. If you fill your mouth with God's word, your life will be very successful. Speak your life into existence; your words are powerful.

Day 30

NO COMPROMISE

> 3 And everyone who has this hope in Him purifies himself, just as He is pure.
> 1 John 3:3

Jesus never compromised in order to win people to the Father. So many ministries and churches are compromising in order to have a large congregation, a large social media base or even to have larger offerings. When Christians compromise everybody loses. Messages are watered down and finely wrapped in dead religion. Compromise will not cause the world to turn to Christ. Only when sin-sick people see us walking in holiness and purity and offering them a way out of oppression, depression and filth, then and only then will they want to know more.

NO COMPROMISE

Day 30

A Wonderful Change

4 Therefore we were buried with Him through baptism into death, that just as Christ was raised from the dead by the glory of the Father, even so we also should walk in newness of life.
Romans 6:4

What should this new life look like? ACCORDING TO THE WORD Jesus declares *"...in my name they will drive out demons they will speak in new tongues they will pick up snakes with their hands, they will drink deadly poison and will not hurt them they will place their hands on sick people and they will get well"* (Mark 16:17-18). You will have a new language, a new power from another realm. You will step into the newness that God has for you. Continue to grow in Grace and allow God to mold you into everything you were meant to be.

Day 31

A Wonderful Change --
By: Ayani_Meli

4 Therefore we were buried with Him through baptism into death, that just as Christ was raised from the dead by the glory of the Father, even so we also should walk in newness of life.
Romans 6:4

Today, think back over the course of the month. We ended on this note about change. There is a popular slogan out these days that espouses that we should, "Be the change." Let God and your relationship with him be the force that drives your change. Are you ready? Imagine your life totally immersed in God. What do you see?

_____
_____
_____
_____
_____
_____
_____
_____
_____
_____
_____
_____
_____
_____
_____
_____
_____
_____
_____
_____
_____
_____
_____
_____
_____
_____
_____
_____
_____
_____

April

By: Stacie Whittaker-Harris

Day 1

Greater Worship Unto Our Great God

5 Exalt the Lord our God, And worship at His footstool-- He is holy.
Psalm 99:5

Rise and Shine, Give God the Glory is the song I hear in my head, as I think about what it means to worship God. Many attribute the lifting of hands, tears, or even words to acts of worship. Others believe worship is soft, gentle, and even quiet. Some believe you can only worship at the church, synagogue, or temple; while others believe you can worship at home, in your car, or while at work. Regardless of your understanding of worship: IT IS PERSONAL. Get Personal with God today!

Now you know that worship is a personal responsibility. It is about personal relationship between you and God. Thus, your charge remains to worship God according to your relationship with Him knowing He is a Great God worthy of Greater worship.

Day 2

Be Mindful of What You Speak

27 He who has knowledge spares his words, And a man of understanding is of a calm spirit.
Proverbs 17:27

Oddly enough, things such as superstitions and old-wives-tales govern not only the way we think, but also the way in which we communicate our thoughts. Most people tend to expend energy on negativity, hopelessness, darkness, and despair (even Believers). These things take shape in the form of our expectations, which ultimately shape our realities. Be mindful of what you think, and even more so, of what you speak.

Today I encourage you to meditate on the scripture above. And, according to Proverbs 18:21, know that you possess the power of life and death. Thus, your charge remains to be aware of the seeds you sow in the form of words, as they are the most powerful tool/weapon ever created.

⟨⟨⟨ **Day 3** ⟩⟩⟩

Seeking The Spirit of God

23 But the hour is coming, and now is, when the true worshipers will worship the Father in spirit and truth; for the Father is seeking such to worship Him. 24 God is Spirit, and those who worship Him must worship in spirit and truth.
John 4:23-24

From sun up to sun down, we allow business and the cares of this world to occupy our mental and spiritual space. We spend time working to make ends meet, caring for our families, and we serve the community fervently. Know that God desires your undivided attention on this day. Thus, your charge remains to seek the Lord while He may be found and submit yourself to the Lord in fellowship, prayer, and worship.

⟨⟨⟨ **Day 4** ⟩⟩⟩

Cling to Love (Pure Love)

9 Let love be without hypocrisy. Abhor what is evil. Cling to what is good.
Romans 12:9

People tend to love their children and express it through gifts. They love their dogs and express it with belly rubs and toy chews. They love their jobs and express it by going each day and working hard. They love their hair and express it by keeping it groomed. Seems as if we use the word "love" fairly loosely.

God so loved us that He gave His ONLY begotten son. Yet, so often, we do not choose to love God in such a way that we consistently demonstrate it in our daily living. Know that to commit evil against your neighbor is, as if, unto God. Thus, your charge remains to pursue peace and cling to love.

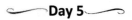 **Day 5**

A Servant's Heart

10 For God is not unjust to forget your work and labor of love which you have shown toward His name, in that you have ministered to the saints, and do minister.
Hebrews 6:10

Throughout the course of the week as you work on your job (or at your business) take inventory of those you encounter. Take notice of their countenance; pay attention to their voices. Also, if by chance someone should smile or laugh and interrupt your quiet meditation—study their presence, take a mental note of what simple thing brought such joy.

Remember, we are all human beings, seeking love and acceptance. I encourage you to preserve your thoughts and find a way to serve those that cross your path and know that a simple act makes the difference. Thus, your charge remains to be selfless, watch, listen, learn, love and serve in love!

Day 6

The Power of Forgiveness

14 For if you forgive men their trespasses, your heavenly
Father will also forgive you. 15 But if you do not
forgive men their trespasses, neither will your
Father forgive your trespasses.
Matthew 6:14-15

About ten years ago my youngest daughter asked if she could hold a butterfly brooch that had been given to me by my mother, before she transitioned from this life. My oldest daughter was shocked that I decided to give the baby girl the brooch to wear that day. At first she told me that it wasn't fair for the youngest to wear the pin because she was not old enough. Then my oldest daughter turned to the youngest and demanded that she cherish it and protect it with her life.

Now, my youngest was known for being clumsy, so the oldest just kept at her about being careful with the family heirloom. When the time came for the youngest to put the pin on her dress, she was so nervous that she snapped it in half. Both girls burst into tears and although I was a little disheartened, I was more concerned about them. I reassured both of them that it was ok, but the oldest scoffed. She adamantly replied that because she had not been given an opportunity to wear the brooch she would never forgive her little sister.

Is there someone you have not forgiven? Why?

_____

_____

_____

_____

_____

Day 7

The Power of Forgiveness — Part 2

> 14 For if you forgive men their trespasses, your heavenly
> Father will also forgive you. 15 But if you do not
> forgive men their trespasses, neither will your
> Father forgive your trespasses.
> Matthew 6:14-15

This short story about a "thing" that was extremely important in my family could have torn my daughters apart, but instead I made it a teachable moment for both of them. I told them that what was most important was that we have memories of my mother. I also told them that God tells us that we must not allow our hearts to be hardened toward others. Therefore, I encourage you to release whatever anger you have toward another and know that God has forgiven you over and over and over and over—and over again more times than you can count. Thus, your charge remains to forgive others as many times as you would like God to forgive you; for there is power in forgiveness.

Day 8

A Faithful Servant

> 24 Only fear the Lord, and serve Him in truth with all your
> heart; for consider what great things He has done for you.
> 1 Samuel 12:24

Eugene worked sixty hours a week for ten years straight. He had a goal in mind so whenever his family asked him to volunteer for the soup kitchen, his excuse was he would be able to do more for "God's people" when he had more to offer them. Prior to this ten-year stint, Eugene faithfully served the soup kitchen with his time, talent as a Chef, and with all the loving smiles he could offer.

After a while, Eugene finally had enough money to purchase his dream home and dream car. He was finally able to travel around the world. Eugene was quite content with all he had and all the work he did, to get all that he wanted. His family came back and asked him to help purchase food for the soup kitchen, but Eugene no longer had the same heart or desire to help "those people." In fact, he believed they needed to stop being lazy and work as hard as he did, in order to feed themselves and their families. Eugene lost sight of what it meant to be a faithful servant.

Today I encourage you to meditate on the scripture above, along with Romans 12:11 which states, *not lagging in diligence, fervent in spirit, serving the Lord.* Therefore, know that if not for God's grace and mercy, you could easily stand in the shoes of the one suffering. Thus, your charge remains to know God has sent YOU to be a vessel of help, love, guidance, support, and service to those in need.

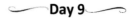 Day 9

His Power, His Strength

> 7 For God has not given us a spirit of fear, but of power and of love and of a sound mind.
> 2 Timothy 1:7

Upon entering the camp, it took the brave, young, newly anointed David only moments to realize that Goliath was no match for the power and strength of the God he served. Most people would think that it was the pebble and sling shot that killed Goliath, but I beg to differ. For me, it was David's resolute faith. From the moment he heard Goliath's boasting and saw Saul's fearful army, he knew what had to be done and he did it without a second thought.

— Day 10 —

His Power, His Strength — Part 2

7 For God has not given us a spirit of fear, but of power and of love and of a sound mind.
2 Timothy 1:7

Conquer your giants with your faith in God's power and strength and know that that is enough. Thus, your charge remains to know who you serve and with that, know His power and His strength! Do not waver!!! Remember: The enemy preys on your fears, for fear is a weakness. Be strong in the Lord!

List the things that have been too hard to accomplish in your own strength and then listen for God's leading on how to get them done.

_____

_____

_____

_____

_____

_____

_____

_____

_____

_____

_____

_____

_____

Come Humbly Before Our God

9 To the Lord our God belong mercy and forgiveness, though we have rebelled against Him.
Daniel 9:9

Around age five I remember vying for the attention of my older brother and cousins and ended up pushed to the ground. My brother, cousins and all their friends laughed at me. I vowed to never forgive my brother and I remember telling my mother the same. My mother told me never to use such a harsh word. She asked me if I loved my brother and I told her not anymore. She then asked me if he loved me and I told her I thought he did until that moment. My mother then asked me if I loved her and of course my answer was yes. She then said that if I truly loved her that I had to love all the parts of her even the bad parts, which included my brother because we both came from her. She told me that it broke her heart to hear me say I did not love my brother.

Then she told me to pray and ask God for forgiveness and go hug my brother; forgiving him the way she forgave me when I messed up. What a great lesson to learn at such an early age. Therefore, know that God is always waiting for you to confess what is in your heart to Him. Thus, your charge remains to come humbly before the Lord our God, knowing He is waiting for you with loving tenderness.

> Forgive others
> as quickly as
> you expect
> God to forgive you.

❧ Day 12 ❧

Faith that Heals

52 Then Jesus said to him, "Go your way; your faith has made you well." And immediately he received his sight and followed Jesus on the road.
Mark 10:52

Two months after giving birth to an almost nine-pound baby girl, I found myself knocking at death's door. I was diagnosed with a chronic illness. At seventeen years of age, I knew enough to trust God to totally deliver me from that horrible sickness. I didn't know how or when, but I believed God was able to do what doctors could not. I suffered seven long years, but I never stopped believing and praying that God would heal my body and restore me back to health. Finally, I went for a follow up procedure and the doctors could no longer find a trace of the illness. Know that your faith makes you whole. Thus, your charge remains to believe and keep on BELIEVING.

❧ Day 13 ❧

Faith In Christ, To Live As Christ

20 I have been crucified with Christ; it is no longer I who live, but Christ lives in me; and the life which I now live in the flesh I live by faith in the Son of God, who loved me and gave Himself for me.
Galatians 2:20

Ever since I was a little girl, I have desired to heal, love, and be like Jesus. My goal was to surrender my total will to God so that I may not be tempted to sin against Him, but my ultimate goal was to walk on water like Jesus. Now of course, I am older and

I understand the Word of God differently. Time and maturity have taught me that to submit to God's control is to have faith that He will lead me. Submission is a developmental process of ridding myself of the will to please the flesh verses submission to please God. Therefore, submit yourself in faith to Christ and know that you can live as Christ. Thus, your charge remains to believe in the power of surrendering your will to God's Will.

Train Up A Child! ⟶ Thaddeus Miles Photography

Day 14

Overcoming Anger

23 But avoid foolish and ignorant disputes, knowing that they generate strife. 24 And a servant of the Lord must not quarrel but be gentle to all, able to teach, patient,
2 Timothy 2:23-24

The older I get the more I realize I do not have to have the last word; nor do I have to win the argument. In fact, less words and more actions are required of me and YOU. Sometimes we don't have to have outside sources to fuel our anger. Look within. Ask Him to show you what the root of the anger is in your life. Once it is revealed to you, ask Him to purge it from your life. Know that YOU are an example of God in the earth. Thus, your charge remains to BE HIS TRUSTED VESSEL, that He may be glorified.

Day 15

Stand: Strong, Courageous, & Faithful

13 Watch, stand fast in the faith, be brave, be strong.
1 Corinthians 16:13

Recently, I relocated to another state. With more than thirty years of living in the same area I grew comfortable with the people, places, and familiar things. I'm sure many of you can imagine the uneasy and uncomfortable feelings I had in starting a new journey in a totally unfamiliar place. However, it was my time for change so I moved forward.

According to Proverbs 3:5-6 we should, *Trust in the Lord with all your heart and lean not on your own understanding; in all your ways acknowledge him, and he will make your paths straight.* Therefore, I exhort you to know that God makes no mistakes. Do not allow yourself to grow complacent due to fear of change.

Thus, your charge remains to: take on that new assignment, start that new business, purchase a home, or simply travel at your leisure. Pray for guidance, make plans, take courage, and trust God in all you do. If the Lord has spoken to you; believe Him at His word and move forward.

Day 16

Acceptable Worship

28 Therefore, since we are receiving a kingdom which cannot be shaken, let us have grace, by which we may serve God acceptably with reverence and godly fear. 29 For our God is a consuming fire.
Hebrews 12:28-29

Pray this today: Our *Father and our King, we exalt you. We give you the highest praise as we meditate on you today. We exalt you. Thank you for the gift of life. We exalt you. Help us to live in a manner that is pleasing unto you. We exalt you. Amen.*

Magnify His Name! What can you praise God for today?

_____
_____
_____
_____
_____
_____
_____
_____

Day 17

Do Not Fear; You Are A Conqueror

8 And the Lord, He is the one who goes before you. He will be with you, He will not leave you nor forsake you; do not fear nor be dismayed.
Deuteronomy 31:8

Trusting God in and through all things seems challenging when health issues arise, when bills overwhelmingly persist, when relationships fail, or when stagnant careers lead to uncertainty, self-doubt, and loneliness. These challenges often induce spiritual and mental decline, which only exacerbates fears of pain, suffering, disappointment, and failure. Self-Abuse through negative self-talk begins to guide decision making processes.

Remember, according to Philippians 4:13, *you can do EVERYTHING through him who gives you strength.* Therefore, know that the gift of today belongs to you. Thus, your charge remains to live a fearless life, knowing with God, you are a conqueror.

Day 18

Hallelujah

7 casting all your care upon Him, for He cares for you.
1 Peter 5:7

Many times we allow the cares of the world to cause sleepless nights. We dwell on past issues or current things that are out of our control. Our mind races too fast and our anxieties spiral out of control. In the daytime, we walk around like basket cases, stuck in our feelings, taking it out on other people and being afraid of the shadows. The enemy has convinced a lot of people that someone is out to get them. Hiding the fact that satan himself is the one out to get them. This is not living according to the Word.

Know that God has your best interest at heart. Thus, your charge remains to walk in harmony with God, allowing Him to carry you through each ordeal. He already knows the outcome and it is in your favor!

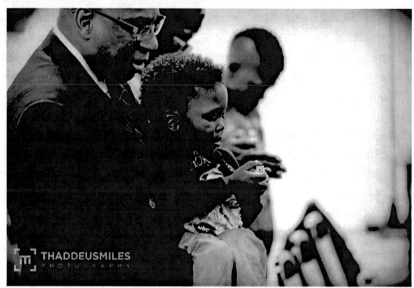

Let Your Father Carry You
Thaddeus Miles Photography

Day 19

Honor and Glory Belong to God

2 Give unto the Lord the glory due to His name; Worship the Lord in the beauty of holiness.
Psalm 29:2

Pray this today: *Father of all creations, today I come before you with a spirit of gratitude. Thank you for molding me into the being I am today. Thank you for your love. Thank you for your grace. Thank you for your mercy. Thank you for keeping me from day to day. I give you all praise!*

God is worthy of all honor. Thus, your charge remains to give glory to the Lord our God in and through all things.

**Day 20**

Characteristics Of Real Love

4 Love suffers long and is kind; love does not envy; love does not parade itself, is not puffed up; 5 does not behave rudely, does not seek its own, is not provoked, thinks no evil; 6 does not rejoice in iniquity, but rejoices in the truth; 7 bears all things, believes all things, hopes all things, endures all things. 8 Love never fails. But whether there are prophecies, they will fail; whether there are tongues, they will cease; whether there is knowledge, it will vanish away.
1 Corinthians 13:4-8

Pray this today: *God of love, it is my desire to be the earthly vessel that you have designed to fulfill the purpose for which you have created me. I pray for strength and courage as I walk with purpose. Use me as a light and servant to draw others to your love, healing, deliverance and kindness. Use me to feed the hungry, clothe the naked, assist the elderly and teach the children. Use the gifts you imparted in me to stir up gifts in others, in Jesus' name, Amen.*

Love is patient; know that God desires to use you as a vessel of love. Your charge remains to share the love of God with every person you come in contact with. Even a smile warms the soul.

**Day 21**

Raising a Generation of Servants

9 As for you, my son Solomon, know the God of your father, and serve Him with a loyal heart and with a willing mind; for

the Lord searches all hearts and understands all the intent of the thoughts. If you seek Him, He will be found by you; but if you forsake Him, He will cast you off forever.
1 Chronicles 28:9

Most people take their titles very seriously. They want to be regarded as Pastor, Doctor, Minister, Evangelist, and so on. One thing most of us forget is our titles do not make us great, but in fact, it is our ability to serve others in a selfless manner that matters most. My friend's father used to state all the time that, ministry is simply service. Therefore, the least is greater. Thus, your charge remains to allow your mind to be renewed in the way that you serve your fellow man. Regardless of whether you are a doctor, lawyer, accountant, grocery store clerk, janitor or judge; honor God with your sincere service to others.

Day 22

Adjust Your View; Adjust Your Faith

27 But immediately Jesus spoke to them, saying, "Be of good cheer! It is I; do not be afraid." 28 And Peter answered Him and said, "Lord, if it is You, command me to come to You on the water." 29 So He said, "Come." And when Peter had come down out of the boat, he walked on the water to go to Jesus. 30 But when he saw that the wind was boisterous, he was afraid; and beginning to sink he cried out, saying, "Lord, save me!" 31 And immediately Jesus stretched out His hand and caught him, and said to him, "O you of little faith, why did you doubt?"
Matthew 14:27-31

Many times in our lives we focus on the "mountains" (obstacles and struggles). We complain about climbing so much that we are unconscious of our ascension to the top. Instead of seeing the sun as our guiding light, we see danger which often lead us to backtrack. We wander aimlessly in valley like places; too afraid to move forward. We do not focus on what is just beyond the mountain, but instead, we remain stuck on the strain we will endure. We grow weary before the journey even begins.

Peter got down out of the boat, walked on the water and came toward Jesus. Some would surmise that he was merely intrigued. It is easy to interpret the scripture that way. Where was faith? Therefore, know that when you remain focused on Jesus, the outcome is always greater than the strain it took to accomplish the task. Thus, your charge remains to be steadfast, take courage, do not waiver, remain fixed on God, and "walk on water" knowing you will NOT sink!

 **Day 23**

A Gentle Love

> 2 with all lowliness and gentleness, with longsuffering,
> bearing with one another in love,
> Ephesians 4:2

One day while I was working in customer service, a man approached me. I asked how I could help. He appeared to be rude, curt, sharp, and condescending. I kept the smile on my face and continued helping him all the way to the end in the same pleasant manner. When we were finished with his transaction he stopped, smiled at me, and reached out to shake my hand. In the handshake he transferred money into my hand. He told me that I handled myself very well and that he appreciated my service.

Today I encourage you to meditate on this scripture. Know that <u>even if they do not announce themselves, people are watching</u>

you (especially children) and possibly testing you. Thus, your charge remains to stand firm as a servant of God; love and serve in gentleness.

Watchful Eyes **Thaddeus Miles Photography**

Day 24

Embrace Humility

11 But he who is greatest among you shall be your servant. 12 And whoever exalts himself will be humbled, and he who humbles himself will be exalted.
Matthew 23:11-12

Humble yourself before the Lord your God. Honor Him with your presence in the world, for you are a light! We talked about love yesterday. Think of love as light. God is love. There is no darkness in Him (1 John 1:5). If God is light and He lives inside of you, you are light. There will not be any hatred, malice, envy or strife coming from you. What is for you is for you; there is

no need to embrace the cutthroat tactics of the world to "get what you want." Know that God gives the increase in due season. Thus, your charge remains to embrace humility.

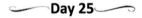Day 25

Be Aware of Mercy

18 Who is a God like You, Pardoning iniquity And passing over the transgression of the remnant of His heritage? He does not retain His anger forever, Because He delights in mercy.
Micah 7:18–19

Pray this today: *God we thank you for your mercy. Now we ask that You help us to be merciful toward our brethren, in Jesus' name, Amen.*

Today, maybe in a big way, maybe in a small way, something will come to challenge this Word. God has extended mercy to you, do the same for your fellowman or woman. Extend some grace, compassion or forgiveness to someone who does not deserve it.

Day 26

The Elect Of God

12 Therefore, as the elect of God, holy and beloved, put on tender mercies, kindness, humility, meekness, longsuffering; 13 bearing with one another, and forgiving one another, if anyone has a complaint against another; even as Christ forgave you, so you also must do. 14 But above all these things put on love, which is the bond of perfection. 15 And let the peace of God rule in your hearts, to which also you were called in one body; and be thankful. 16 Let the word of Christ dwell

in you richly in all wisdom, teaching and admonishing one another in Psalm and hymns and spiritual songs, singing with grace in your hearts to the Lord. 17 And whatever you do in word or deed, do all in the name of the Lord Jesus, giving thanks to God the Father through Him.
Colossians 3:12-17

The scripture today is AWESOME and abundantly clear. I know sometimes you struggle with your identity as a faith filled believer. You may be challenged in your marriage and other relationships. Maybe you are waiting on an answer from God. Maybe you still struggle with that one thing that makes you feel unworthy of God's love, deliverance, protection, grace, and mercy.

WE have struggles from time to time. We lay our burdens down and sometimes we go back and pick them up. What are you currently struggling with?

_____
_____
_____
_____
_____

Day 27

The Elect Of God — Part 2

12 Therefore, as the elect of God, holy and beloved, put on tender mercies, kindness, humility, meekness, longsuffering; 13 bearing with one another, and forgiving one another, if anyone has a complaint against another; even as Christ forgave you, so you also must do. 14 But above all these things put on love, which is the bond of perfection. 15 And let the peace of God rule in your hearts, to which also you were called

in one body; and be thankful. 16 Let the word of Christ dwell in you richly in all wisdom, teaching and admonishing one another in Psalm and hymns and spiritual songs, singing with grace in your hearts to the Lord. 17 And whatever you do in word or deed, do all in the name of the Lord Jesus, giving thanks to God the Father through Him.
Colossians 3:12-17

We have this awesome scripture for a second day! Let me remind you of this one thing: you ARE the elect of the Lord. God has not forgotten you. Continue pressing forward. Thus, your charge remains to KNOW you are the beloved of the Lord! So continue putting on the tender mercies of God, sharing in kindness with humility and meekness. Remember God has already set you free—you are healed and whole!

Day 28

Struggles Produce Greatness

3 we also glory in tribulations, knowing that tribulation produces perseverance; 4 and perseverance, character; and character, hope. 5 Now hope does not disappoint, because the love of God has been poured out in our hearts by the Holy Spirit who was given to us.
Romans 5:3–5

Recently I assessed the last few years of my life and found instances of agony, torment, unforgiveness, bitterness, loneliness and lowliness. These reflections allowed me to remember false smiles which I used to cover some of my deepest issues and pains. I was a young divorced mother with no parents to go to for guidance. I was broken and broken-hearted. I was a survivor of domestic violence, sexual assault, homelessness, and chronic illness.

But I am still standing. Think back over the last few years of your life. Against all odds, what have you withstood?

_____

_____

_____

_____

_____

Day 29

Struggles Produce Greatness — Part 2

3 we also glory in tribulations, knowing that tribulation produces perseverance; 4 and perseverance, character; and character, hope. 5 Now hope does not disappoint, because the love of God has been poured out in our hearts by the Holy Spirit who was given to us.

Romans 5:3–5

Trials come and go, but through it all, things will certainly grow. However, we must be open to continuous self-development and growth. No one asks for hardships or trials, but I have learned more about myself and more about God's expectation of how I treat others. I have developed a deeper compassion toward others and I remember to treat others the way I desire to be treated. Thus, your charge remains not to quit in the midst of struggle, but rather, embrace every moment to grow.

"Is prayer your steering wheel or your spare tire?"

~Corrie ten Boom

Day 30

BE The Greatest Gift

31 And the second, like it, is this: 'You shall love your neighbor as yourself.' There is no other command-ment greater than these.
Mark 12:31

In today's world, chaos appears to be the "new" normal. With constant and countless stories of unnecessary murders, bombings, kidnappings, threats of terrorism, political corruption, broken family structures, lack of educational resources, increased homeless population and so much more, we have become an over sensitized nation. Many are living without regard for human life. Do not become overwhelmed or consumed with the cares of the world and know that God's ever watchful eye desires to see us treat one another according to His word. Thus, your charge remains to free your mind and extend continuous love to your fellow man. Treat your brother/sister with dignity, respect, but most importantly, with LOVE.

May

By: Carla Gaskins

Day 1

Who's Following You In The Valley?

6 Surely goodness and mercy shall follow me All the days of my life; And I will dwell in the house of the Lord Forever.
Psalm 23:6

When you were in the valley ever wonder who was with you. We should be asking who is following us. Going through a rough time alone is not easy. It's the time God wants our attention and to increase our faith. How many times have we cried to others about what we are going through? Key words: "going through." God allowed me to see myself when I was in the valley and when coming out of the valley. Guess what? Something was always there. We are either looking down or looking ahead; we never look back when we are going through.

Why? Glad you asked. Looking back hurts and we can't really see clearly when we look back. If we put things in perspective, we can see the goodness of God. Like the times you had everything you needed and sometimes desired. That was the goodness of God. Then there was the time you didn't die in your sin. That was the mercy of God. When we have the two following us, that is a clear indicator God is with you in that valley of the shadow of death. A shadow does not hurt anyone. In order for a shadow to be produced, there has to be a light source. That light in your valley is the presence of God. The table He is preparing for you now in the presence of those who were waiting to watch you fall is beautiful! Be encouraged today.

Hold on to God no matter what it looks like. It's not over until God says so. Keep your Word before you. It always fights for you and protects you on your journey in and out coming out the valley. Goodness and mercy are following you. That's the best company. Now when you go through the valley again, remember goodness and mercy are your company.

─── Day 2 ───

The Power of the Tongue

21 Death and life are in the power of the tongue, And those who love it will eat its fruit.
Proverbs 18:21

There was a scientist who did a test speaking over water. He spoke words of adoration, love and positive affirmations over one container of water. It produced beautiful crystals when the water was frozen. Speaking positive over something or someone produces positive and beautiful results. Then they spoke words of hate over another body of water and froze it. That container produced deformed and unattractive crystals. Those results were far different from the positive ones.

The way God created the world was with words. It shaped and formed everything the way He spoke it. If we are made in the likeness and image of God, why are we not speaking like Him? Everything He made He completed by saying, "It is good." What words are you speaking? What are they producing? Do you see unpleasantness or beauty in your life? Your words shape your world. If you want to see different results, speak differently. Make a decision today to speak life and not death. Today is a great day to start speaking life.

The human body is 60% water. If you need healing speak life. If your children need to be saved or delivered, speak salvation over them. Speak life and watch the situation change. There is death and life in the power of your tongue. Think on that.

〜〜Day 3〜〜

You Can Not Go Back To Yesterday

1 If then you were raised with Christ, seek those things which are above, where Christ is, sitting at the right hand of God. 2 Set your mind on things above, not on things on the earth.
Col 3:1-2

The question is, can you honestly say that you cannot go back to yesterday? No; you are not who you were yesterday. We must set our minds on the things of God. Seek peace, love, hope and joy. These all come from a place of meditating in the Word of God and prayer. The things of this world are temporary. But the Word is forever and prayer takes us into a place with God.

I am reminded of when I gave my life to Christ. I shared with my friends; they didn't believe me. The natural mind cannot see the spiritual things. How would they know there was a change in me? My life had to match the decision to follow Christ. I had to set my mind on how the Word of God was instructing me to live. I started to change my conversation and how I responded to my old life's triggers

〜〜Day 4〜〜

You Can Not Go Back To Yesterday — Part 2

1 If then you were raised with Christ, seek those things which are above, where Christ is, sitting at the right hand of God. 2 Set your mind on things above, not on things on the earth.
Col 3:1-2

When my friends saw the changes it compelled them to question my new mind, my way of living and my way of thinking. As I was raised with Christ, I saw things from another level that caused me to think higher. My life became a witness for Jesus. God will allow others to see Him through you. Jesus said, *And I, when I am lifted up from the earth, will draw all people to myself.* (John 12:32) What level are you on? Are you focused on the things of the world or the things above? Is your life drawing people to the Jesus you were raised to know?

Take a moment and meditate on it then answer honestly. Meditate on the Word of God today and raise yourself up in Christ Jesus!

Day 5

Holding Fast To Your Confession

23 Let us hold fast the confession of our hope without wavering, for He who promised is faithful.
Hebrews 10:23

Why would God tell us this? There must be something or someone that can steal it. What is your confession today? Is it peace, healing or deliverance from something? The enemy comes expressly to steal, kill or destroy. Walk in your faith to believe God, even when it looks the opposite of what is promised to you. We must know how to be abased and abound. Paul said as much.

The Bible has a great deal to say about contentment. This means being satisfied with what we have, who we are, and where we're going. Jesus said, *Therefore I say to you, do not worry about your life, what you will eat or what you will drink; nor about your body, what you will put on. Is not life more than food and the body more than clothing?* (Matthew 6:25)

—— Day 6 ——

Holding Fast To Your Confession — Part 2

> 23 Let us hold fast the confession of our hope without wavering, for He who promised is faithful.
> Hebrews 10:23

I was both reminded and convicted when I read this. When I was a young girl there were days we had little, if anything, to eat. As I began to grow in the things of God, I started to understand that there will be good days and bad. There would be times of plenty and times of not enough. As a child, I despised the hungry days and the days we had plenty, I was happy. Who wouldn't be?

During the past few days, while focusing on the lean times, I started to feel discouraged. The Holy presence of God showed up and put me in my rightful place. How? I was reminded that I have a safe home, healthy children, and a husband who loves me. My mind is intact and I was about to celebrate my 50th birthday. Everyone cannot say that. Someone, somewhere buried a spouse, has a sick child or is homeless. I should be content in the blessings of God. Whatever the situation God should always get the glory. So, let us hold fast our confession. What is our confession? We can do all things through Christ who strengthens us.

Day 7

Vessels Of Honor

7 But we have this treasure in earthen vessels, that the excellence of the power may be of God and not of us. 8 We are hard pressed on every side, yet not crushed; we are perplexed, but not in despair; 9 persecuted, but not forsaken; struck down, but not destroyed— 10 always carrying about in the body the dying of the Lord Jesus, that the life of Jesus also may be manifested in our body.
2-Corinthians 4:7-10

While having a conversation with someone, bitterness spewed from their mouth; it was grievous. Changing the conversation was not possible, as they became argumentative and hostile. It became very unpleasant to be in their company. My only option was to remove myself from the situation.

Let's take a look at what kind of vessel with which God is pleased. Bitterness can be damaging to you and those around you. The definition of bitterness is resentful cynicism, an intense antagonism or hostility toward others. The Bible teaches us to *let all bitterness, wrath, anger, clamor, and evil speaking be put away from you, with all malice.* It then goes on to tell us how to deal with such bitterness and its fruits by being *kind to one another, tenderhearted, forgiving one another, even as God in Christ forgave you.* (Ephesians 4:31-32)

When we show love toward them we are operating as a vessel of honor. I attempted to show love toward the individual but the determination to spew words of discord continued. All I knew was to pray for that person.

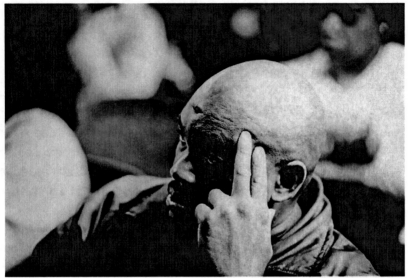

Thinking   Thaddeus Miles Photography

Day 8

Vessels Of Honor — Part 2

**7 But we have this treasure in earthen vessels, that the
excellence of the power may be of God and not of us.
8 We are hard pressed on every side, yet not crushed;
we are perplexed, but not in despair; 9 persecuted,
but not forsaken; struck down, but not destroyed—
10 always carrying about in the body the dying of
the Lord Jesus, that the life of Jesus also may be
manifested in our body.
2-Corinthians 4:7-10**

When you become sharp like an arrow or pungent in your
speech, disagreeable and venomous, you are bitter. Numbers
5:18 states, *the bitter water that brings a curse.* Bitterness
refers to a mental or emotional state that corrodes or "eats
away at" something. Bitterness can affect one experiencing

profound grief or anything which acts on the mind, in the way poison acts on the body. Bitterness allows one to willfully hold onto anger and be ready to take offense.

This is not the life God intended for you; we are to be loving and kind. The treasure that the scripture speaks of is the Holy Spirit of God. The excellence of His power is there to keep us from being crushed or destroyed. It's to make us better vessels, not bitter ones. When you think of treasure you think value. What do you value more? Pleasing God or your quest to be bitter?

Yes, life may have thrown some fiery arrows or even knocked you down. If you are in Christ, you have that treasure in you. Use it to become a better you. Don't allow the enemies of the world to make your company undesirable. You are more than what life has done to you.

Day 9

The Unconditional Yes To Jesus

> 15 So when they had eaten breakfast, Jesus said to Simon Peter, "Simon, son of Jonah, do you love Me more than these?" He said to Him, "Yes, Lord; You know that I love You." He said to him, "Feed My lambs." 16 He said to him again a second time, "Simon, son of Jonah, do you love Me?" He said to Him, "Yes, Lord; You know that I love You." He said to him, "Tend My sheep." 17 He said to him the third time, "Simon, son of Jonah, do you love Me?" Peter was grieved... Lord, You know all things; You know that I love You." Jesus said to him, "Feed My sheep.
> John 21:15-17

Have you ever wondered what it would be like to hear Jesus ask, "Do you love me?" I never really paid attention to the number of times Jesus questioned Simon Peter. Jesus asked and gave three similar commandments. It brought up the question of Jesus' omniscience. Why ask the same question over and over? Simon Peter answered, "Yes" three times; it was really for him. Jesus told him initially, "you will deny me three times" and Peter said he wouldn't. He denied him three times. I believe Jesus wanted Simon Peter to understand that even after the denials, he could be used. Simon Peter was being called to a purpose even after denying Jesus.

Do you or have you felt like you let God down after following Him? Knowing who He is and what He has done for you?

_____

_____

_____

_____

_____

⌁ Day 10 ⌁

The Unconditional Yes To Jesus — Part 2

15 So when they had eaten breakfast, Jesus said to Simon Peter, "Simon, son of Jonah, do you love Me more than these?" He said to Him, "Yes, Lord; You know that I love You." He said to him, "Feed My lambs." 16 He said to him again a second time, "Simon, son of Jonah, do you love Me?" He said to Him, "Yes, Lord; You know that I love You." He said to him, "Tend My sheep." 17 He said to him the third time, "Simon, son of Jonah, do you love Me?" Peter was grieved... Lord, You know all things; You know that I love You." Jesus said to him, "Feed My sheep.
John 21:15-17

Jesus has an unconditional love He wants to impart into us. We just have to recognize it and listen to God's leading questions. In spite of our wrong, He loves us and has a work for us to do. Just because He asked three times, did not mean He didn't believe Simon Peter. He wanted Simon Peter to realize and embrace that His love for him was unconditional. Simon needed to recognize that his love for Jesus is the same love he must have to lead; which is required of him in order to say yes to the calling of leading the people.

Jesus instructed, "Feed my lambs, tend my sheep and feed my sheep." In order to do that, Simon Peter had to go from the brotherly love he held for Jesus, to the unconditional love of Jesus, to do what he was called to do. That calling was to lead the people.

Don't think for one moment, that because you messed up, He cannot use or desire to use you. God already factored in your messing up. Conviction will always cause you to turn your heart back to Jesus. Is it in you to answer, "Yes Jesus I love you" and walk in the call on your life? Listen to the voice of God; He may be asking you the same question and the answer should be yes.

 Day 11

Your Walls Are Coming Down Today

1 Now Jericho was securely shut up because of the children of Israel; none went out, and none came in. 2 And the Lord said to Joshua: "See! I have given Jericho into your hand, its king, and the mighty men of valor.
Joshua 6 1-2

Because of whose you are, the enemy wants to keep you away from what God has promised. Jesus came that you may have life and have it more abundantly. That life includes prosperity. The enemy will try to make you believe you will never come out of poverty and sin. What is your Jericho right now? Who is hindering your ability to live the life God has for you? The enemy wants you and everything that belongs to you locked up. Make a decision today that the walls must come down. We must ask God for His strategy. God told Joshua, "see, I have given you Jericho." In that statement God allowed Joshua to see the gates locked and the guards walking around the city. They were not allowing anyone in or out. That was proof to Joshua that the very ones inside the city knew God would take it and give it to them. <u>That is a powerful revelation</u>!

Anytime someone does not want you to have something of value, they will lock it up. The enemy always wants what belongs to someone else. He has a grip on your promise and your future. Will you just sit and allow it? I can just see the fear they had of the people of God, only because they knew the reputation of God. All that God had done, all of the battles the people overcame, caused fear in them. Every time you break through something, the enemy will add more security and more soldiers. Not because he is afraid of or can stop God, but it is to intimidate you and to make you change your mind about what God promised you. God will allow it, to increase your faith. He will show you what is yours first, I believe, to get you ready for the process. Understand that what He gives is so grand, the warfare will be intense; however, it's no match for God. Everything connected, even to the ownership of something that belongs to God, will be given to you. God will give you favor and cause a reverential fear of the God in you. It's time to tear down the Jericho walls in your life today.

Binding & Loosing
In Jesus Name

Matthew 18:18

Day 12

Binding and Loosing

17 Jesus answered and said to him, "Blessed are you, Simon Bar-Jonah, for flesh and blood has not revealed this to you, but My Father who is in heaven. 18 And I also say to you that you are Peter, and on this rock I will build My church, and the gates of Hades shall not prevail against it. 19 And I will give you the keys of the kingdom of heaven, and whatever you bind on earth will be bound in heaven, and whatever you loose on earth will be loosed in heaven."

Matthew 16:17-19

Every morning on my way out, the same problem persists; I can never find my car keys. I even have a hook and chain that will allow me to attach them to my purse. I never take full advantage of that hook's purpose. Once I was so frustrated, I just said a short one sentence prayer. *Lord help me find my keys.* I walked to the other side of the bedroom, moved my pajama's and the keys were there. Have you found yourself looking for something that will unlock your life, to move you forward? Well, Matthew 16:19 has the answer. Reading this gave me revelation of something else. When God gives us revelation on something, it gives us the keys and access to that which was revealed. You have the ability and power to lock it and or release it.

Are you taking full advantage of the purpose of the Word of God in your life?

_____

_____

_____

_____

_____

Day 13

Binding and Loosing — Part 2

17 Jesus answered and said to him, "Blessed are you, Simon Bar-Jonah, for flesh and blood has not revealed this to you, but My Father who is in heaven. 18 And I also say to you that you are Peter, and on this rock I will build My church, and the gates of Hades shall not prevail against it. 19 And I will give you the keys of the kingdom of heaven, and whatever you bind on earth will be bound in heaven, and whatever you loose on earth will be loosed in heaven."
Matthew 16:17-19

Years ago God gave me revelation on how to unlock my womb to conceive. Fibroid tumors were the very things that caused me not to conceive. He revealed to me how to pray for healing in the area of conceiving. When God revealed the strategy of praying for myself, I became pregnant and gave birth to a beautiful daughter. Whenever I prayed for someone that desired to have a child, they conceived. I have been given the keys to bind the spirit of infertility, rendering it useless in the earth and in the heavenly realm. I also have the power to loose fertility to move in its purpose, to bring forth fruit in the earth and for that fruit to produce in the heavenly ream. Whatever you need in life, ask God to reveal the keys so that you can operate in revelation. God's revelation gives you the dominion over and in the area for which He has given you the keys. Whenever you are binding something there must always be a loosening of something. Just make sure your binding and loosing causes good fruit to come forth. Ask God for revelation concerning you today. *Watch Him move and give you authority over that which holds you bound!*

Day 14

Feeding Your Flesh Will Cost You Everything

30 And Esau said to Jacob, "Please feed me with that same red stew, for I am weary." Therefore his name was called Edom. 31 But Jacob said, "Sell me your birthright as of this day." 32 And Esau said, "Look, I am about to die; so what is this birthright to me?" 33 Then Jacob said, "Swear to me as of this day." So he swore to him, and sold his birthright to Jacob. 34 And Jacob gave Esau bread and stew of lentils; then he ate and drank, arose, and went his way. Thus Esau despised his birthright.
Genesis 25:30-34

The Word of God tells us we are the seed of Abraham; Isaac was the first born to Abraham. In that day, the birthright went to the first born. Esau was the first born and Jacob was the second. Jacob was a deceiver and deceived his brother under the instruction of his mother. There is always something behind the scenes to rob you of your birthright and influence you to give it up. Esau gave up his birthright to satisfy his flesh, when he was weak and his brother took advantage of him. Being weak and not understanding fully what his birthright entailed, he sold it for a bowl of stew, just to satisfy his flesh. Esau despised his birthright and gave up a legacy that his brother clearly understood. He gave up double of everything his father had for him. His brother understood, just like satan understands, the blessings of God more than we do.

What have you given up? What promises did God give you, that you have allowed the enemy to take and have dominion and ruler-ship over your life?

_____

_____

_____
_____
_____
_____

Day 15

Feeding Your Flesh Will Cost You Your Everything — Part 2

30 And Esau said to Jacob, "Please feed me with that same red stew, for I am weary." Therefore his name was called Edom. 31 But Jacob said, "Sell me your birthright as of this day." 32 And Esau said, "Look, I am about to die; so what is this birthright to me?" 33 Then Jacob said, "Swear to me as of this day." So he swore to him, and sold his birthright to Jacob. 34 And Jacob gave Esau bread and stew of lentils; then he ate and drank, arose, and went his way. Thus Esau despised his birthright.
Genesis 25:30-34

Adam and Eve forfeited their inheritance of Eden for a piece of fruit. Let that resonate in your Spirit for a moment. The enemy went to the weaker of the two and ultimately deceived them both to give up dominion, ruler-ship and fellowship with God. Marriages are destroyed because someone was weak and gave in to satisfy their flesh. Sometimes folks get weak in their mind and succumb to suicide. <u>What you feed the most will win</u>. Feed your spirit with the Word of God; His promises are yes and amen. If you gave up your rights to anything or anyone you have no one to blame but yourself. Esau blamed his brother for deceiving him. When we do not understand the blessings of God, we will treat it like junk mail or a huge burden. Strengthen yourself in the Word of God, His promises and His will for your life.

⟶ Day 16 ⟶

Encouragement For The Warrior

15 And he said, "Listen, all you of Judah and you inhabitants of Jerusalem, and you, King Jehoshaphat! Thus says the Lord to you: 'Do not be afraid nor dismayed because of this great multitude, for the battle is not yours, but God's.
2 Chronicles 20:15

As a warrior you walk in great power and authority. How you tread must be taken seriously. Some battlefields you must not go onto unless you are skilled for that battle. I never fight alongside someone that does not show their scars. Scars are proof you survived; reminders of what did not kill you!

I am not saying boast about them; just be proud of what you came through. All battles are not yours. Choose wisely and it is a must to consult with God first. The authority and power you walk in are thunderous to your enemy and its response is to attack defensibly. Again, all battles are not yours; knowing which ones are yours, with God on your side, will produce victory.

Pray this today: *Father, teach my hands to war in the spirit of prayer. Do not allow me to succumb to my flesh, as there is no good thing with it. Give me strategy to have victory in every field I am destined to take back. Give me wisdom to know when the battle is yours and the unction to step back and allow you to be God. Father, I pray that your Word will be in my heart to speak with authority and power, over every situation that tries to overtake me and rob me of my faith to trust you in all things, in Jesus' name. Amen*

Day 17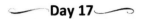

In His presence

11 You will show me the path of life; In Your presence is fullness of joy; At Your right hand are pleasures forevermore.
Psalm 16:11

This morning, God ministered to me "right where I was." There is nothing like the ministry of God. A huge smile broke out on my face and I laughed heartily. I had no idea what was going on until I fully understood Psalm 16:11. When you are in the presence of God there is fullness of joy, unspeakable joy. The presence of God is sweet and overwhelming; it envelopes you like a blanket.

Are you in need of the presence of God? Are you in need of love, peace and joy? I implore you today to read the scripture and seek God for understanding and revelation; seek Him for an experience you have never had before with Him.

The fullness of God will fill every void you have. He is the great I AM. Whatever you need Him to be today, He is that when you are in His presence. No matter what is going on around you, it disappears when you are in His presence. You become full and experience everything—He is a healer, protector and provider. It's a place of refuge. Seek Him, I promise your experience will be heavenly.

Write your own short prayer. Seek Him.

_____
_____
_____

_____
_____
_____
_____
_____

~~~A Heavenly Experience~~~ Isaiah 40:28-31
Thaddeus Miles Photography

~~~Day 18~~~

Rest

1 A Psalm of David. The Lord is my shepherd; I shall not want. 2 He makes me to lie down in green pastures; He leads me beside the still waters.
Psalm 23:1- 2

God's Word will cause you to rest in it. The Word is rich and never exhausted. The Word of God is fresh and sweet. While in green pastures, sheep receive nourishment and green grass to

lie in and to eat. We should always be looking to the Word of God to feed our hungry souls. The Word should always be a place of rest, as there are people who desire rest and peace. They would give anything for it but they refuse to lie down and accept Jesus and the Word of God. However, those of us who have Jesus, can be led by the Spirit of God. Then, we have that "leading beside the still waters," which is the peace of God's Holy Spirit. That silence is golden. It's the leading of God's sweet Spirit, like still waters running deep. God's leading will always be accompanied with peace. He leads us to the place where He wants us to reside. Trust Him today, to lead you to a place to gather what you need for your journey.

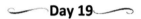 Day 19

Prayer Of Forgiveness

16 Be of the same mind toward one another. Do not set your mind on high things, but associate with the humble. Do not be wise in your own opinion. 17 Repay no one evil for evil. Have regard for good things in the sight of all men. 18 If it is possible, as much as depends on you, live peaceably with all men.
Romans 12:16-18

Pray this today: *Father, I come in the name of Jesus. I ask for a fresh commitment to you. I desire to live a life of peace and harmony. Not only with other brothers and sisters of the body of Christ but also with friends, associates, business partners, neighbors and family.*

Father I repent of holding onto bad feelings toward others. I turn myself to Godly repentance and loose myself from bitterness, resentment, envy, strife and unkindness in any form. Father I ask for your forgiveness and I believe that you have forgiven me. By faith I receive it, having the assurance that I am clean from all unrighteousness through Christ Jesus. Father I ask that you forgive and release all who have wronged me. I forgive and release them. Father I ask that your mercy and your love and kindness be extended to them. From this moment on I will walk in love to seek peace and live in agreement with your Will for my life. I will be kind to others in a manner that is pleasing to you, that I may be in right standing with you Father. I ask that your ears are attentive to my prayers. It is said in your Word that the love of God has been poured out into my heart, by the Holy Spirit who is given to me. I believe Father that love flows into the lives of everyone I know, that we may be filled with the fruits of righteousness. I pray that it brings glory and honor unto You Lord and I thank you now Father for all that You have done concerning this prayer, in Jesus' name, Amen.

Day 20

What Does Your Fruit Look Like?

22 But the fruit of the Spirit is love, joy, peace, long-suffering, kindness, goodness, faithfulness, 23 gentle-ness, self-control. Against such there is no law.
Galatians 5:22-23

Last night, my daughter came to me and said sadly, "Mommy I don't know what I look like without my glasses." I thought that was strange. The look on her face was heart breaking. She was very disappointed, so I asked her to take off her glasses. "Let me take a picture of you then put your glasses on and you will see clearly what you look like without your glasses," I said. She grinned when she was able to see her face clearly. Her remark was I look like you and daddy. Most people will see her with me and say, "she looks like you." But when her father shows up she looks exactly like him and no longer looks like me.

I received a great revelation in her dilemma. When we get in the presence of our Heavenly Father and begin to worship, we look like who He created us to be, in His Image and in His Likeness. He sees us differently than the way we see ourselves. Is the fruit of the Spirit working in your life, for people to see your heavenly Father's Image and Likeness upon you? Do you show love, joy, peace, kindness, goodness, faithfulness, gentleness and self-control? Take a look at your fruit, evaluate it. Your desire should be to look like our Heavenly Father.

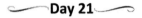Day 21

Dressed For War Prayer

10 Finally, my brethren, be strong in the Lord and in the power of His might. 11 Put on the whole armor of God, that you may be able to stand against the wiles of the devil.
Ephesians 6:10-11

Speak this affirmation and prayer today: *In the name of Jesus, I put on the whole armor of God; that I may be able to stand against the wiles of the devil. For I wrestle not against flesh and blood but against principalities, powers the rulers of the darkness of this world and spiritual wickedness in high places. Therefore, I take unto myself the whole armor of God, that I may be able to withstand in the evil day and having done all, to stand. I stand therefore having my loins girt about with truth. Your Word Lord, which is truth, contains all weapons of my warfare, which are not carnal but mighty through God, to the pulling down of strongholds.*

My breastplate of righteousness is faith and love. My feet are covered with the preparation of the gospel of peace. In Jesus, I have peace and I pursue peace with all I am. I am a minister, reconciling and proclaiming the good news of the gospel. With the shield of faith, I am able to quench all the fiery darts of the wicked. The helmet of salvation holds my thoughts, my feelings and the purpose of God's heart. The sword of the Spirit, which is your Word God, comes against all trials, tests, temptations and tribulations. They are cut to pieces. The plans of the enemy are struck down as I speak the Word of God. Greater is He that is in me, than he that is in all the world. I thank you for my armor today. I pray over every occasion and every season. I pray in the spirit; my power and my ability and sufficiency are from you God, who has qualified me as a minister and a dispenser of a new covenant. I pray, in the name of Jesus, Amen.

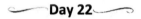 **Day 22**

The Great Intercessor Prayed

John 17

Today's devotional is short so that you can read the entire chapter of John 17. It holds great knowledge and revelation. In this chapter you can see how our Lord and Savior shifted in prayer from being an intercessor, to Christ the Anointed One. Then He moved into son-ship and prayed as a leader for the disciples. The last shift found Him praying as our Lord and Savior for all of us, who would believe the word and come into salvation. He also prayed for those that will believe in the future.

How does this make you feel?

_____

_____

_____

_____

_____

_____

 **Day 23**

The Great Intercessor Prayed — Part 2

John 17

Your salvation was wrapped in the prayers of Jesus thousands of years ago. Prayer is a very intimate communication between man and God; it's a place where you can hear from God and make your request known to him. Our will in prayer must match the Will of God for our lives. What is the Will of God? It's His Word Jesus prayed as an intercessor for Himself, first. If you ever thought it selfish to pray for yourself then think again! Jesus set the example in John 17, verse 1. *Jesus spoke these words, lifted up His eyes to heaven, and said: "Father, the hour has come. Glorify Your Son, that Your Son also may glorify You.*

I want to encourage you today to pray for yourself. Pray for those who God has given you charge over and pray for those who do not know Jesus for themselves. Pray that they may come to know Him as Lord and Savior. Prayer is very essential to your existence! Ask God for your own revelation on prayer. Let John 17 be your Word of meditation on today. Selah.

 **Day 24**

Power!

20 Now to Him who is able to do exceedingly abundantly above all that we ask or think, according to the power that works in us,
Ephesians 3:20

There is a power that is working in us. That power is in harmony with heaven and earth. The power that works in us is God. God is obligated to take care of what belongs to Him. Have you noticed whenever you have less than what you need to operate or to accomplish His purpose, God will come and do more than you could ever ask or think? God is so big and so vast that whatever He does is big and not small.

When has God shown Himself BIG in your life?

_____

_____

_____

_____

_____

_____

_____

_____

_____

_____

_____

_____

_____

Day 25

Power! — Part 2

20 Now to Him who is able to do exceedingly abundantly above all that we ask or think, according to the power that works in us,
Ephesians 3:20

I remember a time when I was unemployed and had very little money to pay all the bills and fulfill the necessities of life. I had more during that time of my life, than I had when I was employed. That can happen, whenever we have to totally depend upon God. That is a time that our faith should increase to trust God. Desiring for us to have more than enough, He becomes THAT exceedingly, abundantly, above all we ask or think. What exactly does that mean? I believe there is a time when God reveals Himself as an overflow. The exceedingly and abundantly is actually the overflow of God. Just imagine that you are living in an overflow you haven't really tapped into. Anything recognized as the exceedingly and abundantly has now become the overflow. Think about a full glass of water that ran over. You are in the portion that ran over. We can shout off that revelation alone! So when you start to think it's you making it happen, think again. It's the POWER of God working in you.

Day 26

What Are You Building?

8 By faith Abraham obeyed when he was called to go out to the place which he would receive as an inheritance. And he went out, not knowing where he was going. 9 By faith he dwelt in the land of promise as in a foreign country, dwelling in tents with Isaac and Jacob, the heirs with him of the same promise; 10 for he waited for the city which has foundations, whose builder and maker is God.
Hebrews 11:8-10

I am reminded of the people of Babel. They came together with one united mind to build a tower to the heavens. God did not instruct them to do that and ultimately He caused the people to scatter. Are you doing something without the instructions and directions of the Master Architect? God wants us to see Him as a solution to a problem. He wants to reveal His plan for our lives; we make plans that do not include God. When they fall apart, we wonder why it didn't work. I tried for years to host a women's event and it either never came together or it failed. I was frustrated and wanted to give up on ministry all together. But when I sought God in prayer for His plans for my life, I hosted my first successful women's conference. Lives were changed and it opened doors for me I was never able to open. My heart and passion was there but God was not included. Step back and look at your plans. If you can't see God in it, I suggest you either walk away from it or seek Him as the basis. What you build is temporary but what God builds lasts for eternity.

Pray this today: *Father, forgive me for focusing on my own plans and dreams. Help me to seek you for guidance in all that I do, in the name of Jesus, Amen.*

Day 27

Does God Cry?

9 In all their affliction He was afflicted, And the Angel of His Presence saved them; In His love and in His pity He redeemed them; And He bore them and carried them All the days of old.
Isaiah 63:9

I felt a weeping in my spirit one morning at 4:30 a.m. and I had no real reason to do so. I asked God was that Him weeping? Then I wondered. Does God cry?

The Word of God says He does cry. I believe God cries. In Romans 8:26, it says that when we don't know what to pray for, God the Holy Spirit *intercedes for us through wordless groans.* I believe God groans more than words can express and God cries more than tears can show. We simply cannot comprehend it all.

The Bible shows that Jesus wept over the grave of Lazarus and He wept over the city of Jerusalem. Jesus felt the dark absence of God when He cried and He said, ...*My God, my God, why have you forsaken me?* (Mark 15:34) I believe such a God cries over a broken world and cries with all of us.

The Old Man – He has seen much!
Thaddeus Miles Photography

Day 28

Does God Cry? — Part 2

9 In all their affliction He was afflicted, And the Angel of His Presence saved them; In His love and in His pity He redeemed them; And He bore them and carried them All the days of old.
Isaiah 63:9

So God, through the Holy Spirit, groans along with us and with creation. And God, through Jesus on the cross, suffers our pain and feels injustice and the oppression of evil. We do not have a God who is untouched by human suffering. We do not have a malicious God, sitting heaven, pulling strings and playing dice with human lives. No. We have a God who groans with us and who suffers with us.

From this perspective, I have to change the "why" question from "Why did this happen to us?" to "Why did this happen to us and God?" Because God feels our pain and suffering, we are now also asking why did God allow Himself to suffer, when He has the power to prevent it? Let's remember we are not the only ones that hurt—so does God. What we see in the world not only make us cry, but God also cries.

Day 29

Have No Fear

> 9 Have I not commanded you? Be strong and of good courage; do not be afraid, nor be dismayed, for the Lord your God is with you wherever you go.
> Joshua 1:9

There was a post on social media, during football season, about Michael Vick. The post mentioned that how after many years people continue to protest his playing football. There was mention of how he was a dog killer and many other slanderous words. God sent an amazing revelation and the scripture Joshua 1:9 came to mind. God commanded us to not be afraid. He is with us always. My question was how is it that Mr. Vick can get on the field knowing people still hate him? Resilience was the answer. He pushes past the hate and murmurs of those that want to destroy him. God has redeemed his life from all wrong doing.

From what has God redeemed you?

_____

_____

_____

_____

_____

Day 30

Have No Fear — Part 2

9 Have I not commanded you? Be strong and of good
courage; do not be afraid, nor be dismayed, for the
Lord your God is with you wherever you go.
Joshua 1:9

God's word will do that for you. We are not to fear anyone
when we walk with God! It makes you tough, strong,
irrepressible and quick to recover. They are offended by His
resilience. The enemy hates you, when you don't give up or give
in. He always hides behind something to camouflage the real
reason, which is hate. When you have God on your side you
walk with a spirit of resilience. Nothing and no one can invoke
fear. Today be strong in the Lord; God has not given the spirit
of fear but of love and a sound mind.

Continue to trust God and remain resilient.

Day 31

Today is different. Write everything that is on your heart. Every
desire, need, goal, and past hurt. Once you have written it, just
begin to thank God that it is done, finished, corrected, erased
or set into motion. Watch Him do it!

June

By: Bernice Loman

Day 1

Seek Him First

33 But seek first the kingdom of God and His righteousness, and all these things shall be added to you.
Matthew 6:33

There are a lot of things that go on within a day. As soon as we awake, there are chores, there is work, school, children, and other things that scream for our attention. With all of that, we still have to pray, read our Bible or find some form of inspiration. There seems to not be enough time in the day for all of that. Yet God behooves us to *seek ye first the Kingdom of God.* So this lets us know that seeking Him and His righteousness first is vital. Not just seeking Him alone is enough, it has to be first. Before we start our day, let's seek Him first and trust that ALL other things will be added. Rising early in the morning helps!

Day 2

Don't Give Up!

9 And let us not grow weary while doing good, for in due season we shall reap if we do not lose heart.
Galatians 6:9

Ever felt like you tried all you knew to do? You prayed, fasted, gave up some things that you knew were wrong, and so on. Yet, you felt defeated? It's the middle of the year and you still haven't accomplished what you hoped? I challenge you to not give up! Don't grow weary of well doing. <u>You shall reap.</u> It's not the end of the year yet. Expect some miracles to happen.

Day 3

Expect The Best

8 Finally, brethren, whatever things are true, whatever things are noble, whatever things are just, whatever things are pure, whatever things are lovely, whatever things are of good report, if there is any virtue and if there is anything praiseworthy--meditate on these things.
Philippians 4:8

What are you thinking? Are you thinking on pure, holy and things of good value? If not, change your way of thinking and expect God's best for you. Have you ever heard, "we are what we think?" Well, it's true. All of us are where we are today because of what we thought. You may be in a situation where you don't want to accept responsibility for your actions. Pray and find allow God to reveal to you how to change it. Do your due diligence to walk out the rest of the day believing, praying, and trusting that if His best is not already yours, expect to walk into it.

Day 4

What Do You Say?

21 Death and life are in the power of the tongue, And those who love it will eat its fruit.
Proverbs 18:21

The Word also says, *now when the tempter came to Him, he said, "If You are the Son of God, command that these stones become bread." 4 But He answered and said, "It is written, 'Man shall not live by bread alone, but by every word that proceeds from the mouth of God.' " (Matthew 4:3-4)*

What did you say when you lost your job? What did you say when your loved one became sick? Think about it. Did you speak death or life? Make sure that you aren't in the place that you are in because of the words that came out of your mouth. If you are not saying what God said, it is death. Whatever God speaks is Life. He is Life. Think about every situation that you are in now, take a moment and speak the Word to it. When the enemy came to Jesus to tempt Him, Jesus spoke "It is written..." Are you speaking what is written in the Word of God?

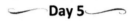 **Day 5**

What Did He Say?

> 15 Be diligent to present yourself approved to God, a worker who does not need to be ashamed, rightly dividing the word of truth.
> 2 Timothy 2:15

Do you remember the last time you were in a disagreement? You tried your best to give your point of view. Well, if what you say is right, you will try your best to speak the truth and believe nothing else. When the enemy comes, he comes to kill, steal and destroy. You have to be prepared to speak God's Word as Jesus did in Matthew 4. Guess what? If you don't know the Word, it's hard to speak the Truth to the enemy. That's why God tells us to study His Word. You can't use what you don't know, correct?

What has God told you? What should you tell the enemy?

_____

_____

_____

_____

_____

Day 6

You Are Not Going To Drown

25 Then His disciples came to Him and awoke Him, saying, "Lord, save us! We are perishing!" 26 But He said to them, "Why are you fearful, O you of little faith?" Then He arose and rebuked the winds and the sea, and there was a great calm.
Matthew 8:25-26

You too can rebuke the strong wind and waves of your life. Speak God's Word to the storm, "Peace be still." Don't live in the storm being afraid of everything. Fear can cause our situations to overshadow us. Begin to speak to the storm with faith and expect the Peace of God to show up! Jot down your fears. Now, rebuke them out of your life!

_____
_____
_____
_____
_____

Day 7

On The Right Side

6 And He said to them, "Cast the net on the right side of the boat, and you will find some." So they cast, and now they were not able to draw it in because of the multitude of fish.
John 21:6

Have you ever felt like all your hard word was ineffective? I've been there. It's a terrible feeling to work all your life only to feel like nothing has been accomplished. Jesus' disciples were trying to catch fish all night and caught nothing. It wasn't until they obeyed God and cast their net on "the right side," that they were successful. Are you on the left side (obeying your flesh)? Be obedient to God and cast your net on the right side.

⸺ Day 8 ⸺

I Am The One

10 Thus Jesse made seven of his sons pass before Samuel. And Samuel said to Jesse, "The Lord has not chosen these."
1 Samuel 16:10

Think to yourself, and mean it, *I am the One*! While Samuel was looking for a king, Jesse presented seven of his sons. While he didn't consider David, Samuel told Jesse "the Lord hasn't picked any of these." Samuel called for the other one—the eighth son. Are you the eighth one? Are you the one that God has called? You may feel like you aren't strong enough; maybe you feel weak. God's Word states in 1 Corinthians 1:27, *But God has chosen the foolish things of the world to put to shame the wise, and God has chosen the weak things of the world to put to shame the things which are mighty.* Do not feel that God will never use you. You are the eighth one that God wants to use for His glory!

⸺ Day 9 ⸺

Can He see your Faith?

5 When Jesus saw their faith, He said to the paralytic, "Son, your sins are forgiven you."
Mark 2:5

Are you in doubt? As you read Mark 2:1-5, understand that a sick man was unable to get to Jesus, so others near him opened the roof and let him in. When Jesus saw their faith, He healed him and forgave his sins. Ask yourself, is my faith active? Have I surrounded myself with people who are active and radical in their faith? The Bible made mention of the faith of the companions! This means that the faith of those connected to you has a huge impact on your life. Can you also imagine how important it is for you to believe God for yourself? Take a moment to reflect on things that you need to trust God for today. Have faith!

_____

_____

_____

_____

_____

_____

_____

_____

_____

_____

Day 10

Is God On Your Schedule

1 A Psalm of David when he was in the wilderness of Judah. O God, You are my God; Early will I seek You; My soul thirsts for You; My flesh longs for You In a dry and thirsty land Where there is no water.
Psalm 63:1

David said, "Lord I earnestly search for you" meaning, he sincerely searched for God. When we are truly hungry for God, we begin to add Him to our daily routine. We should not wait till think we have time, we should search for Him before our

daily schedule gets loaded; search for Him throughout the day and night. Matthew 6:33 states, *but seek ye first the kingdom of God, and his righteousness; and all these things shall be added to you.*
Day 11

Lord, Send Your Angels!

43 Then an angel appeared to Him from heaven, strengthening Him.
Luke 22:43

When Jesus was faced with a monumental task, an angel from heaven came and strengthened Him. Are you faced with trouble, an enormous task or a trial? If so, ask the Lord to send His angels to strengthen you. Oftentimes when we go through, it feels like we are the only one going through. It seems like at that very moment, everyone around us is happier and we're the only one suffering. Not so; we all go through at times. The good news? We have angels available to strengthen us through the journey.

Be not forgetful to
entertain strangers,
for thereby, some have
entertained
Angels unawares.
Hebrews 13:2

Entertaining Angels Unawares
Thaddeus Miles Photography

Day 12

The Second Time Around

1 Now the word of the Lord came to Jonah the second time, saying, 2 "Arise, go to Nineveh, that great city, and preach to it the message that I tell you." 3 So Jonah arose and went to Nineveh, according to the word of the Lord...
Jonah 3:1-3

God had already given Jonah an assignment to go to Nineveh; but he was disobedient. However, God gave Jonah instructions a second time. If you read the story, you will notice the result of his disobedience. After the hardships Jonah faced, he finally went to Nineveh. Think of something God has told to do but disobedience and fear have blocked you. If you are reading this, it means that God has given you a second chance to get it together. Where is the place that God has asked you to go? Is it another city? Did He tell you to start a business? Did He tell you to start a conference and preach to the broken-hearted? Today, pray for God's strength to carry you through this task. Thank Him for giving you a second chance and be obedient this time!

Day 13

Don't Follow The Wrong Advice

9 Now when much time had been spent, and sailing was now dangerous because the Fast was already over, Paul advised them, 10 saying, "Men, I perceive that this voyage will end with disaster and much loss, not only of the cargo and ship, but also our lives." 11 Nevertheless the centurion was more persuaded by the helmsman and the owner of the ship than by the things spoken by Paul...
Acts 27:9-22

It's your turn to search the scriptures. You will find the centurion was given a warning by Paul, that the ship was going to be damaged. Sadly, he didn't listen. He later discovered that Paul was correct. Are you following the wrong advice? Are you ignoring the warnings of God? God sends people to help keep us away from danger. It's up to us to make the wise decision. The good news? Today is a new day! Make up your mind that you will follow the right advice and live a peaceful life.

— Day 14

Can He See Your Faith?

5 When Jesus saw their faith, He said to the paralytic, "Son, your sins are forgiven you."
Mark 2:5

Let's revisit this scripture again. FAITH IN ACTION IS AMAZING. Jesus healed the sick man based on the faith of others, who had enough courage to bring him to Jesus. Evaluate who you have in your inner circle. Do they believe? Their faith can cause healing in your situation. Take another moment and examine their character. Does doubt rule their lives? Share this story with them and how important it is to have a faith-filled friend. When you get discouraged, their faith can be the vehicle that helps facilitate your miracle. Most importantly, can God see your Faith? Do you believe that HE can do the impossible?

— Day 15

God Will Provide

6 The ravens brought him bread and meat in the morning, and bread and meat in the evening; and he drank from the brook.
1 Kings 17:6

God will make a way for you. Receive this no matter what your situation looks like. God knows how to send what we need just when we need it. Are you willing to believe this? Jot down everything you need God to do for you. Now, declare faith over each of them. Watch the results.

_____
_____
_____
_____
_____
_____
_____
_____
_____

Day 16

"Use What U Got"

7 Then she came and told the man of God. And he said, "Go, sell the oil and pay your debt; and you and your sons live on the rest."
2 Kings 4:7

I like to believe that this story is based on obedience. In spite of the widows' condition, she obeyed Elisha and gave what she thought was her last. By her obedience, she received more. She gained more simply by using what she had.

How can you learn from this? Think of the long list of things you want to have and the short list of things you may have. Take those things you have and ask God to show you how to use it to the max. God is able to multiply what you have.

Day 17

The Light

16 No one, when he has lit a lamp, covers it with a vessel or puts it under a bed, but sets it on a lampstand, that those who enter may see the light.
Luke 8:16

Do you know how valuable you are to the world? I know you may feel like you have a long way to go with your spiritual walk but God has you! What little you know, God can use. You are a light of the world. Stop covering the light and let it shine. Let others see the light in you. Start that blog you've been wanting to share. Create that prayer group or event you've thought about. There is a group of people that are waiting on your light.

SALT Light
Matthew 5:13-16

Day 18

On The Right Side

6 And He said to them, "Cast the net on the right side of the boat, and you will find some." So they cast, and now they were not able to draw it in because of the multitude of fish.
John 21:6

I have been like those fishermen; doing things repeatedly and becoming discouraged when the results were the same. Do you find yourself frustrated wanting a different outcome? How about asking God to help you! Don't go another day without asking Him what His plans are for your life, business, ministry, etc. You may be doing it your way and not HIS.

~~~Day 19~~~

Take it God; It's Yours

29 Take My yoke upon you and learn from Me, for I am gentle and lowly in heart, and you will find rest for your souls.
Matthew 11:29

Let God take the BURDEN. STOP holding onto what happened years ago, even yesterday. Examine your thought patterns. A lot of times, we are stressed because we are holding on to the memories of the past. You may have said "I let it go," but what about your inner feelings and thoughts? Let it go! Give your burdens to God. He cares for you and is always available. Tell HIM!

~~~Day 20~~~

I Can Do It

13 I can do all things through Christ who strengthens me.
Philippians 4:13

Today is a new day. What defeated you yesterday, will not defeat you again. Affirm this in your mind every day. With God, you can do it! Take your mind off the obstacles and please stop looking at how someone else did it. Rely on the strength of God to get you through this. Jot down your list, pray and move with faith and the strength of God!

_____

_____

_____

_____

_____

Day 21

Love

13 And now abide faith, hope, love, these three; but the greatest of these is love.
1 Corinthians 13:13

Out of faith, hope and love, love is the greatest gift. Love seems to have been forgotten in this cold world. Guess what? God (who is Love) is still available. Don't go another day without embracing Love and sharing it. Take a moment. Pray and ask God to show you how and who you can show love to today.

Day 22

Working For The Good

28 And we know that all things work together for good to those who love God, to those who are the called according to His purpose.
Romans 8:28

Romans 8:28 is one of my favorite scriptures. It has encouraged me many times during tribulations. This is one of those scriptures that you must remember. It will be your strength during hard times. No matter what place you are in your spiritual walk, there are some not so great days. Maybe today is one of the good days. That's wonderful! Remember this scripture and share it! Say this, "It is working for my good!"

Day 23

Keep God's Word In Your Mind

3 You will keep him in perfect peace, Whose mind is stayed on You, Because he trusts in You.
Isaiah 26:3

Have you noticed how easily we can be distracted? The mind can shift quickly. You ever thought about how you had to pay one bill, then your mind is flooded with bills? The next second depression sets in. I've been down that road and will not go again. God says keep our mind on Him and it will keep us in perfect peace. This means, let go of the worries of bills, sick loved ones, failures, etc. and keep your mind on HIM. Think about all He has done, is doing and will do. Enjoy His peace!

Day 24

You Are Forgiven

9 If we confess our sins, he is faithful and just and will forgive us our sins and to cleanse us from all unrighteousness.
1 John 1:9

When you confess your sins to God, He is faithful and justly forgives you for all your sins. Get this scripture in your spirit. Many times we stumble and feel so defeated because of our sins. Confess them and move on. You are forgiven! Don't stay in the state of defeat. Ask the Holy Spirit to help guide you in all truth. Also, when faced with someone who has wronged you, remember you too have to forgive; as God forgave you.

"Oh God!   Thaddeus Miles Photography

Day 25

Another Day/New Mercies

23 They are new every morning; Great is Your faithfulness.
Lamentations 3:23

Move on! It's another day and God's mercies are new every morning. Embrace change and don't bring yesterday into your day. Ask God what would He would like for you to do today. Listen for His instructions for the new day.

Day 26

The Renewed Mind

12 rejoicing in hope, patient in tribulation, continuing
steadfastly in prayer;
Romans 12:12

I have to share another one of my favorite scriptures. I will include content about the mind often, because I believe that once our mind is made up and renewed, everything else falls in place. We are not to be conformed to the ways of this world, but be transformed by the renewing of our minds. Transformation cannot come without a renewal of the mind. Many times we seek transformation without a new mind. It cannot happen. Ask the Holy Spirit to help you! We can renew our mind with the Word of God. I don't want you to think that you just need to take a few seconds and read a scripture and go back to your previous mindset. No, this renewal should take place daily. Ask the Holy Spirit each day for transformation.

Day 27

Cut It Off

2 Every branch in Me that does not bear fruit He takes away; and every branch that bears fruit He prunes, that it may bear more fruit.
John 15:2

What dead things in your life have you been trying to hold on to? If it doesn't produce life, cut if off. Don't let it hold you back any longer. You are a tree that needs to continue to grow. There is much greatness in you and you can't be hampered by unfruitful branches. Those unfruitful branches can be old friends, old habits, old thoughts, etc. Cut them off!

What do you need to cut off?

_____
_____
_____
_____
_____

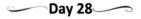 **Day 28**

Don't Go Until He Speaks

8 And the Lord called Samuel again the third time. Then he arose and went to Eli, and said, "Here I am, for you did call me." Then Eli perceived that the Lord had called the boy. 9 Therefore Eli said to Samuel, "Go, lie down; and it shall be, if He calls you, that you must say, 'Speak, Lord, for Your servant hears.' "... 10 Now the Lord came and stood and called as at other times, "Samuel! Samuel!" And Samuel answered, "Speak, for Your servant hears." 11 Then the Lord said to Samuel: "Behold, I will do something in Israel at which both ears of everyone who hears it will tingle.
1 Samuel 3:8-11

We all need to be just like Samuel, to listen carefully for God's voice and not move until we hear Him. We can learn from reading 1 Samuel 3 that when God speaks, it's not always about us but for someone else. God showed Samuel, Israel. What has God shown you specifically? Don't ignore the soft voice or signs again. He is speaking to you. Listen and allow Him to use you. Yes, He can use you. Say, "Use me Lord."

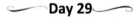 **Day 29**

Don't Wait For The 2nd Letter, Do It Now!

1 Dear friends, this is now my second letter to you. I have written both of them as reminders to stimulate you to wholesome thinking.
2 Peter 3:1 NIV

Paul wrote another letter to remind the church of the Lord's return. How many times do we need to be reminded of His coming? He is coming back for us. Let us be ready now. Repent daily. Don't worry about yesterday. Remember, today is a new day with new mercies. Welcome the Holy Spirit into your daily walk to help you prepare for the Lord's coming.

> Acts 3:19 "Repent therefore, and turn back, that your sins may be blotted out."

Day 30

Keep On Building

15 And it happened, when our enemies heard that it was known to us, and that God had brought their plot to nothing, that all of us returned to the wall, everyone to his work.
Nehemiah 4:15

We all have a work and purpose on this earth. God didn't just decide to breathe life into us—just because. There is something we are on this earth to do or accomplish. When you discover your purpose, you will find that there will be many distractions. What I LOVE about the story of Nehemiah is that when the people were faced with opposition, they kept building. Is there something you need to do but have become distracted? Perhaps you gave up because of sickness, lack of funds or support. Did you allow opposition to divert your focus? It's time to keep building.

July

By: Tabitha Vinson

Day 1

Stand Firm

3 He shall be like a tree Planted by the rivers of water, That brings forth its fruit in its season, Whose leaf also shall not wither; And whatever he does shall prosper.
Psalm 1:3

Today marks the first day, of the seventh month, of the New Year; an opportunity to be planted firmly in our dreams and allow your hands to manifest long awaited prosperity and bring it into full maturation.

What are your dreams? What are you standing firmly on (or believing for)?

_____
_____
_____
_____
_____

Day 2

Our Enemy Must Be Present

5 You prepare a table before me in the presence of my enemies; You anoint my head with oil; My cup runs over.
Psalm 23:5

It's a necessity for enemies to be present. The main purpose is for God to brag on us and about us naturally, as he has already done spiritually. You see, your table not only displays the answered prayers but much more. Rejoice in the fact that He's

literally taken off of your enemies' tables those very desires they wanted; however, they can't have them because it's been transferred over to your table.

──── Day 3 ────

Trust Me

7 Jesus answered and said to him, "What I am doing you do not understand now, but you will know after this."
John 13:7

In our darkest hour, we must trust Jesus no matter what. In the eye of the storm, there's a calm and a peace that surpasses natural understanding. This is where our trust needs to remain intact; for when it's finally over we will discover we've been qualified to handle the massive blessings that await us.

──── Day 4 ────

Independence

36 So if the Son sets you free, you will be free indeed.
John 8:36

Being free in Christ marks our independence from the enemy's snares and traps. We must stand firm and decree our independence from captive situations and watch the Spirit of Deliverance move into action.

This season of independence, reflect on the following picture. What does it speak to you about freedom? Situations in your life may make you feel like you are pinned down. Develop some tunnel vision and look at things through a God filter. Mr. Miles' photo "Small Window, Big Picture" speaks to me. Our

freedom is rooted in God and He is showing you your freedom through that window. The window symbolizes following Him.

Small Window, Big Picture
Thaddeus Miles Photography

Day 5

He Knows

**8 Record my lament; list my tears on your scroll—
are they not in your record?
Psalm 56:8 NIV**

Every tear we shed is collected; for each drop writes a chapter in our book that He reads every day. So be comforted in this one thing: for every disappointment and challenge we face be assured He knows.

Day 6

I Am Baal Perazim

> 20 So David went to Baal Perazim, and David defeated them there; and he said, "The Lord has broken through my enemies before me, like a breakthrough of water." Therefore he called the name of that place Baal Perazim.
> 2 Samuel 5:20

When King David was fighting against the Philistines, he was exposed to another facet of God's character. He learned that God is the *Master of Breakthroughs*, which is the meaning behind Baal Perazim. When we're faced with a Philistine challenge, call on the Master of Breakthroughs. For as He delivered the enemy into David's hands, so will God cause us to triumph over our enemies.

Day 7

Poof They're Gone

> 7 The Lord will cause your enemies who rise against you to be defeated before your face; they shall come out against you one way and flee before you seven ways.
> Deuteronomy 28:7

Although our enemies outnumber us, remember they are still clearly outmatched. For when God is for us, who can really stand against us? It's interesting the number seven is used in this passage, as it is a divine number representing completeness. How comforting it is to know that when God scatters them He does this completely for they are no longer seen.

Day 8

Compassionate Christ

35 Jesus wept.
John 11:35

We are to remember that Christ is a compassionate Savior. He feels every pain and disappointment that we encounter. Never allow the enemy or any naysayer to tell you there's no Christ; to say that He is nowhere to be found or doesn't care. For this simple verse reminds us of His tender heart toward His children.

Day 9

He Laughs

13 The Lord laughs at him, For He sees that his day is coming.
Psalm 37:13

We need to be reminded that the Lord has a great sense of humor; especially toward those who do evil against us. Those who commit such an infraction have started the time table for their demise, as the Wrath of God will soon strike. God laughs at our enemies. Just when they think they've won, God causes them to fall greatly because of their own folly. Be comforted and know that our God is one who is about to strike on our behalf.

Day 10

God's Got It

19 Beloved, do not avenge yourselves, but rather give place to wrath; for it is written, "Vengeance is Mine,

I will repay," says the Lord.
Romans 12:19

Don't take matters into your own hands; it's easier said than done. When we truly learn to forgive the offense, that's when God becomes our defense. That's the true meaning behind this verse. Be comforted in knowing that God, regardless of how long it might take, will handle the matter better than we ever could.

Tell God what you need for Him to handle today!

_____

_____

_____

_____

_____

Day 11

Strong Fortress

1 Hear my cry, O God; Attend to my prayer. 2 From the end of the earth I will cry to You, When my heart is overwhelmed; Lead me to the rock that is higher than I. 3 For You have been a shelter for me, A strong tower from the enemy.
Psalm 61:1-3

What a comfort to know that when we converse with God, He not only listens, but becomes a shield. When we are faced with a dilemma, He becomes a rock for our feet to stand on and a shelter in our time of need. Regardless of what may come, when we call upon the true and living God, He becomes the barrier between us and the circumstance we're facing.

Day 12

Jehovah Mekoddishkem

13 "Speak also to the children of Israel, saying: 'Surely My Sabbaths you shall keep, for it is a sign between Me and you throughout your generations, that you may know that I am the Lord who sanctifies you."
Exodus 31:13

As Christians, we know our walk is never easy and are aware of the various trials and tribulations; however, we must keep in mind there's a reason behind such "tests." In truth it's a process of sanctification and during these times we are introduced to Jehovah Mekoddishkem, which means The Lord sets you apart. We're being set a part for something greater that will be revealed once we've graduated from the process. Be comforted in knowing that although it might not feel good, in the end there will be a great reward not only in heaven, but on earth as well.

Day 13

In the Beginning

58 Jesus said to them, "Most assuredly, I say to you, before Abraham was, I AM."
John 8:58

We know that Christ existed long before Abraham, but how many times do we forget that He also existed long before Lucifer and all the angels? Be comforted in knowing that God the Creator WAS (in our finite understanding of existence) before Lucifer and the angels; this provides reassurance that creation, more succinctly the demonic realm, can never outwit or overshadow the Creator. This is a fact that's been established from the very beginning.

— Day 14 —

Joint Power

17 and if children, then heirs--heirs of God and joint heirs with Christ, if indeed we suffer with Him, that we may also be glorified together.

Romans 8:17a

As Christians we are joint heirs with Christ and being joint heirs gives us the right to trample over the enemy. All are His creation, but not all are His children. Be comforted in knowing that having a relationship with God makes you a joint heir; and being in the family, that gives you certain rights and privileges that creation doesn't.

Prayer Works! — Thaddeus Miles Photography

Day 15

Press toward Destiny

14 I press toward the goal for the prize of the upward call of God in Christ Jesus. 15 Therefore let us, as many as are mature, have this mind; and if in anything you think otherwise, God will reveal even this to you. 16 Nevertheless, to the degree that we have already attained, let us walk by the same rule, let us be of the same mind.
Philippians 3:14-16

As Christians, that which is good and pure and would be a shining example of the good life through Christ, the enemy would do everything in their so called power to thwart. However, we must fight! We must also press toward that high calling for the sake of establishing the kingdom of God on earth and to show the lost there are benefits to serving the true and living God.

Day 16

Preservation

23 Now may the God of peace Himself sanctify you completely; and may your whole spirit, soul, and body be preserved blameless at the coming of our Lord Jesus Christ. 24 He who calls you is faithful, who also will do it.
1 Thessalonians 5:23-24

Just like the most precious and exquisite fine art is under the watchful eye of the curators at The Louvre, so are we, the children of the Living God, forever under His watchful eye. He's more than a Father; He's a Dad that's ever so close if we just remember that He is faithful to protect, and preserve His kids.

Day 17

Be Confident

6 being confident of this very thing, that He who has begun a good work in you will complete it until the day of Jesus Christ;
Philippians 1:6

Christ called us from the darkness into the light. He began this work in each of us and be assured that, beyond a shadow of doubt and despair, regardless of what things may look like, He will perfect His work. Despite the challenges we face, Christ will complete with absolute certainty all the things He started. The thing about Christ, He doesn't give up on us and we dare not give up on HIM.

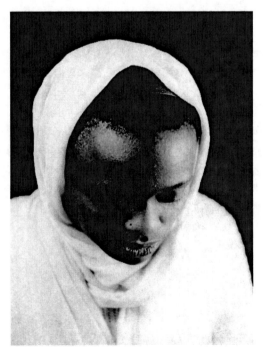

Seeking Him — Thaddeus Miles Photography

⟵Day 18⟶

Already Done

30 So when Jesus had received the sour wine, He said, "It is finished!" And bowing His head, He gave up His spirit.
John 19:30

The moment Christ died, the exchange of power took place. No more does the enemy have power over the Children of the Marvelous Light. Granted, he is slick, but the God we serve is greater and has empowered us to outwit anything the enemy tries. We must embrace the power that's been given to us.

⟵Day 19⟶

Speak Life!

21 Death and life are in the power of the tongue, And those who love it will eat its fruit.
Proverbs 18:21

Often this verse is quoted with the word "life" first, but notice the Scripture reads with "death" being the first word. Be sober and diligent to remember that we must enforce a cease and desist order on our tongue and speak only life; for our sinful nature would prefer to speak death first; i.e., talk about the problem rather than focus on the solution. It's time for us to reprogram our tongue and speak life first!

Day 20 ⟶

You're the Seasoning

13 You are the salt of the earth; but if the salt loses its flavor, how shall it be seasoned? It is then good for nothing but to

be thrown out and trampled underfoot by men.
Matthew 5:13

Lots of recipes call for salt, whether iodized or sea. Most of the time this particular seasoning is part of our cooking regimen. From the spiritual standpoint we are the seasoning for the lost. We are to add flavor to the lives of those who are searching for that ONE answer. Through our life we can lead them to the ultimate chef, who is none other than Christ. We must not allow our seasoning to grow stale.

⌇⌁Day 21⌇⌁

Kingdom Within

21 nor will they say, 'See here!' or 'See there!' For indeed, the
kingdom of God is within you.
Luke 17:21

Not only are we the salt of the earth, we are the Kingdom of God. It's through us that we are to establish on earth what is already established in Heaven. Count it an honor and privilege to establish a palatable and divine kingdom on earth.

⌇⌁Day 22⌇⌁

Pay Attention

14 For God may speak in one way, or in another,
Yet man does not perceive it.
Job 33:14

God does speak; however, not always in the same manner. We must attune our spiritual ears to be receptive to what He says and does. In doing so we're able to avoid the snares of the enemy. What do you hear him saying today?

_____

_____

_____

_____

_____

～～ Day 23 ～～

What's In My Heart?

9 For the eyes of the Lord run to and fro throughout the whole earth, to show Himself strong on behalf of those whose heart is loyal to Him. In this you have done foolishly; therefore from now on you shall have wars.

2 Chronicles 16:9a

We need to ask ourselves, "What's in my heart?" This will be the start of a purging of those things we need to expunge from the four chambers (spiritually) in order for God to fully take up residence. Thus, we are guaranteed the LORD will be our guard and defend us.

～～ Lord Where Are You? ～～ Thaddeus Miles Photography

Day 24

It's Only a Dream

3 As a dream comes when there are many cares, so the speech of a fool when there are many words... 7 Much dreaming and many words are meaningless. Therefore, stand in awe of God.
Ecclesiastes 5:3, 7

At times we have bad dreams. Sometimes it is the result of what we eat, stress of life or failing to meditate before we lay down. Be assured that when God speaks to us during our sleep state, His message is clear and memorable—don't fear anything else, for it was only a dream.

Day 25

Pray the Word

11 So shall My word be that goes forth from My mouth; It shall not return to Me void, But it shall accomplish what I please, And it shall prosper in the thing for which I sent it.
Isaiah 55:11

When we remind God of His Word, we know assuredly that what we pray He not only hears us, but will carry out the very thing we prayed about; for He watches over His word and will fulfill it at the appointed time.

Day 26

Everything We Need

2 The Spirit of the Lord shall rest upon Him, The Spirit of wisdom and understanding, The Spirit of counsel and might, The Spirit of knowledge and of the fear of the Lord.
Isaiah 11:2

As Christians we tend to forget certain aspects of Christ's nature or persona. We know Him as our Perfect Savior, and that He loves us unconditionally; however, how often do we forget that the seven spirits rest upon and within Christ? Holy Spirit, Wisdom, Understanding, Counsel, Might, Knowledge and Reverence all make up the persona of the Christ. After all, did not Christ say, "I and the Father are one?" Since that's the case we truly have everything we need in Him.

Day 27

I Got the Power

8 But you shall receive power when the Holy Spirit has come upon you; and you shall be witnesses to Me in Jerusalem, and in all Judea and Samaria, and to the end of the earth.

Acts 1:8a

This is the promise given to every Christian, the power of the Great Comforter; the Holy Spirit, who is in actuality the Mind of God. The Holy Spirit is the great nemesis of the demonic realm. The Spirit rests in our subconscious to protect us while we're sleeping; resides also in our conscious when we're awake to order our steps and even in our unconscious state for that is where we became a new creature. Yes, the Holy Spirit occupies all three aspects of our consciousness; for that reason alone, each one of us can shout, "I Got the Power!"

Day 28

Another Filling

31 And when they had prayed, the place where they were assembled together was shaken; and they were all filled with the Holy Spirit, and

they spoke the word of God with boldness.
Acts 4:31

We need to remind ourselves there's one baptism, but many fillings of the Holy Spirit. Meaning as we grow in Christ, we need to be filled with more of His Spirit in order for our flesh to die. Last year's anointing will not help with today's issues. As we're elevated in the kingdom we need to follow the cue of our predecessors by praying for another filling of His Spirit.

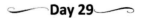 **Day 29**

Core Friends

1 After six days Jesus took with him Peter, James and John the brother of James, and led them up a high mountain by themselves. 2 There he was transfigured...His face shone like the sun, and his clothes became as white as the light...3 Just then there appeared before them Moses and Elijah, talking with Jesus... 9 As they were coming down the mountain, Jesus instructed them, "Don't tell anyone what you have seen, until the Son of Man has been raised from the dead.
Matthew 17:1-3, 9

In this journey called life we need people who we can trust. This level of trust is exclusive only to the very small core of our inner circle. We can have many friends, but only a few can be called ride or die friends. They are the core who will stand by you through thick and thin; correct you when you're wrong and love you even when you get into arguments. At times the core doesn't consist of family, but people who will share in the burden of our trials, rejoice in our plans and cheer us on in our accomplishments. As we go higher in the realm of the spirit we need to ask ourselves, "Who are my core friends?"

Day 30

Can You Hear?

11 Then He said, "Go out, and stand on the mountain before the Lord." And behold, the Lord passed by, and a great and strong wind tore into the mountains and broke the rocks in pieces before the Lord, but the Lord was not in the wind; and after the wind an earthquake, but the Lord was not in the earthquake; 12 and after the earthquake a fire, but the Lord was not in the fire; and after the fire a still small voice.
I Kings 19:11-12

When the Prophet Elijah was on the mountain he stood and marveled at the demonstration of God. He heard and saw the mighty wind, the earthquake and the fire, but in all this God was not there. In that moment of silence, it was then that Elijah heard the great *I AM* in a still small voice. The question we need to ask ourselves, "Can we hear Him too?"

Day 31

Amen

14 And to the angel of the church of the Laodiceans write,'These things says the Amen, the Faithful and True Witness, the Beginning of the creation of God:
Revelations 3:14

I'll Bet you didn't know another name for Christ is The Amen? This should provide us with additional insight and encouragement that we're not only opening our prayers using "In the name of Jesus" or "In Jesus name," but sealing our prayers with His other name—<u>Amen</u>.

August

By: Tamika and Mark J. Avery

Day 1

An Ordained Season

**1 There is a time for everything, and a season for
every activity under heaven:
Ecclesiastes 3:1**

Today, we encourage you to take the time to think about where
you have *come from*, but also think about *where* God is leading
you.

Once you come to the realization of who and what God is, it
brings about change. Instead of fighting change, we encourage
you to accept it for what it is: transition. Just as every season
of the year will not be your favorite, every season of your life
will not be as well received as others.

Expecting summer to last 12 months is foolishness. Praying for
year round winter would be ridiculous. Yet, how often have we
prayed for a lifetime of joy, happiness, and good times; wishing
that God would spare us completely of tears, sadness, and
pain? We assure you, as summer transitions into fall, the
seasons of our lives will transition as well.

Every season has a purpose and is necessary! Every season
depends on the others to bring out its full potential. You could
never appreciate the beauty of Spring without a long cold
Winter. Fall would cease to exist without summer. This is God's
design and it is beautiful.

No matter what the situation or circumstance you are dealing
with right now, know that God is omniscient, omnipotent, and
omnipresent. God is always in control of the seasons, naturally
and spiritually. Instead of trying to find a way out of your

season, ask God what it is He would have you learn, while you are in it. Trusting that everything has a season and a time, give praise for the joy and the pain, the sadness and the laughter in your life and thank God that He is ordering the seasons in your life, as the foundation for your future!

—— Day 2 ——

What's Changed?

17 Therefore, if anyone is in Christ, he is a new creation;
the old has gone, the new has come!
2 Corinthians 5:17

Anything that was created is considered to be a creature (a created thing). That is hardly worth mentioning on its own, so why bring it up? We have been creations of God since birth but this scripture is telling us that somehow, without changing in any tangible way, we are different. Obviously, this leaves questions. How are we different? When did we change?

It is confusing for the world because the transformation is spiritual. Christ took our sins upon Himself, leaving us clean and new. Accepting this and following God's teachings, truly means that our old sin-filled ways (mindsets, perspectives, beliefs, habits, tendencies, etc.) have passed away. We may be the same height, weight, complexion, etc., but we are no longer the same creations of God that we used to be.

We are "new" creatures. We abide by a different set of rules. It is no longer "our" will, but "God's" Will be done. The change from being "in" Christ is completely different from any change that comes from "knowing" of Christ. We need an intimate relationship with God; He cannot just be in our heads. We have to have Him in our hearts. God has to be leading and we have to be following!

Day 3

How Can I Rest?

28 "Come to me, all you who are weary and burdened, and I will give you rest. 29 Take my yoke upon you and learn from me, for I am gentle and humble in heart, and you will find rest for your souls. 30 For my yoke is easy and my burden is light."
Matthew 11:28-30

I heard people quote these scriptures repeatedly, until I knew them by heart, without ever having read them. Yet, those same people were troubled, tired, and still burdened. They were Christians being run ragged by the problems of this world. I did not understand how these verses could be so simple and so untrue at the same time.

It was eventually revealed to me that though the verses are simple, they are frequently misunderstood. Coming "unto" Jesus is often confused with coming to the church. The "rest" He promises is "unto your soul" not necessarily directly for your body, mind, or from your problems. His yoke being easy is not the same as not having a yoke at all and His burden being light is not the same as having a life with no problems, pain, or struggle.

These scriptures invite those that have never known Christ, as well as those that have wandered away from Him, to connect to Jesus and allow Him to help us find the peace that God has always wanted for us. It is not always easy, but it is always as simple as Him saying, "Come," and us replying, "Yes."

Day 4

Vanity! All Is Vanity!

1 The words of the Teacher, son of David, king in Jerusalem: 2 "Meaningless! Meaningless!" says the Teacher. "Utterly meaningless! Everything is meaningless."
Ecclesiastes 1:1-2

Ecclesiastes is considered a book of wisdom, along the same lines as Proverbs and is authored by arguably one of the wisest men to ever live. He opens this book by saying that everything is vanity. What does vanity mean? Ultimately, it means believing that something or someone is more than what they really appear. Sometimes we tend to become vain and place our trust in ourselves or worldly things, rather than in God.

Solomon spends the next twelve chapters in Ecclesiastes expounding on that opening statement. Along the way, he covers alcohol, money, power, youth, work, joy, pain, entertainment, and all things under the sun; explaining that while each has its season, each is still vanity. Depending on how you read it, Ecclesiastes can come across as depressing and hopeless. If everything is truly vanity, as Solomon so delicately states it, then why bother with anything? Why are we even here? Much less, why bother even writing or reading a book about strengthening our walk with God?

This daily devotional is not ending on a sour note. Just leaving room for you to reflect. What do you hope to gain from strengthening your walk? We will conclude this tomorrow.

_____

_____

_____

_____
_____
_____
_____
_____

Day 5

Vanity! All Is Vanity! — Part 2

1 The words of the Teacher, son of David, king in Jerusalem: 2 "Meaningless! Meaningless!" says the Teacher. "Utterly meaningless! Everything is meaningless."
Ecclesiastes 1:1-2

Why bother even writing or reading a book about strengthening our walk with God? The answer lies in the last two verses of the last chapter of the book. Solomon tells us in Ecclesiastes 12:13-14, *Let us hear the conclusion of the whole matter: Fear God and keep His commandments, for this is man's all. For God will bring every work into judgment, Including every secret thing, Whether good or evil.* This is why we should bother. This is why we are here; why we need to strengthen our walk with God.

There are only two types of things in existence. That which is eternal and that which is not eternal. Anything and everything that is not eternal is vanity, while that which is eternal is all that matters. Our duty is to fear God and keep His commandments. How often are we guilty of believing otherwise? How often have we allowed meaningless things to consume our time, energy, and resources? Strengthening our walk with God often begins with realizing or sometimes remembering what is truly important. It was true for Solomon. It is true for us. We suspect it is true for you as well.

Day 6

Who Do You Think You Are?

> 1 The LORD said to Job: 2 "Will the one who contends with the Almighty correct him? Let him who accuses God answer him!"
>
> Job 40:1-2

How blasphemous is it for an imperfect creation to correct a perfect creator? How arrogant is it to complain to an omniscient, omnipotent, omnipresent God that He is mishandling something or being unfair? Sometimes I think we forget who is God and who is not. Sometimes we get so caught up in ourselves and thinking that we run things that we forget that God is our creator and we are His creation.

The book of Job goes into deep detail about how Job was upright, yet God asked the devil, "have you considered my son Job?" While many see Job's story and say that it teaches us about how God blessed Job and how he received "double for his trouble," we think the book teaches a different lesson.

If God's "point" in the story was to simply give Job more worldly things, He could have done that at any time and without the decimation of Job's life. It, also, does not seem likely that God's purpose was to teach satan a lesson, as he is not mentioned after the second chapter of the book and the climax of the story revolves around God talking directly to Job about His greatness. That is where the point is. That is seemingly why the book was written.

God spent four chapters educating Job, about who is God and who is not. God engineered and controlled the situation to bring Job, to a point where he could receive this lesson into his heart. He wanted Job to not only recognize, but accept His full sovereignty over all of creation. Although, we think that what Job was forced to endure was terrible, God deemed it necessary and Job thanked Him for it, in the end, even before any of his wealth had been restored. A wise person learns from the mistakes of others. I pray that we are wise enough to learn Job's lesson through our own trials and maybe avoid his.

─── Day 7 ───

Stand Still and See God's Glory

40 Then Jesus said, "Did I not tell you that if you believed,
you would see the glory of God?"
John 11:40

This scripture comes just before Jesus raises Lazarus from the dead. Jesus had just been told repeatedly that "if" He had come earlier; Lazarus would not have died. In essence, Mary and Martha, two of Jesus' closest friends and fiercest believers were still doubting or not comprehending the power of God.

That statement could inspire a book. Often we can't see the glory of God because we don't believe Him (take Him at His word). We can't get out of the struggle because we are busy trying to figure out why it is happening. It is so easy to say, "I trust God," but our question is "Do you really trust God?" Will you not believe until you see the nail prints in His hand?

Expound: Do you really trust God?

_____
_____
_____
_____
_____

— Day 8 —

Stand Still and See God's Glory — Part 2

40 Then Jesus said, "Did I not tell you that if you believed, you would see the glory of God?"
John 11:40

Mary and Martha both recognized that Jesus could have kept Lazarus from dying, but did not understand that God is not limited by death, or any other circumstances, for that matter. Jesus actually took His time getting there to illustrate this point. He knew that everyone would believe once the miracle had taken place, but how much greater would it have been for them to believe before the miracle happened? How much better would it be to understand that God has no limits, before He proves it to us?

Our circumstances are temporary, God is eternal. Our struggle is fleeting, God is everlasting. Our tears are finite, God is infinite. So many times we attempt to limit God to events, just as those that mourned Lazarus did. Eventually God will prove His omnipotence to us. We are better off believing because we were told, than because we have been shown.

— Day 9 —

Perfect Peace

3 You will keep him in perfect peace, Whose mind is stayed on You, Because he trusts in You.
Isaiah 26:3

We do not know of an easy way to say this, so we will just be bluntly honest. When we are worried, concerned, scared, tense, distressed, etc., it is most likely because we are not concentrating on God. We have allowed what we are going through or dealing with to distract us. We are focusing on what we see, rather than God and His promises. We need to turn our focus to God because we cannot change life no matter how much we worry about it. So, instead, we should keep our mind on God and trust Him. The bible says let not your heart be troubled if you believe. The question is, do you believe? Is God not capable? Is God not in control?

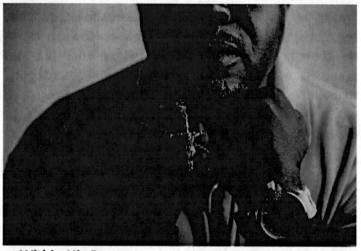

Within His Power ⟶ Thaddeus Miles Photography

Day 10

Perfect Peace — Part 2

> 3 You will keep him in perfect peace, Whose mind is stayed on You, Because he trusts in You.
> Isaiah 26:3

Notice that this is actually a two-part scripture. Isaiah states two things will keep us in perfect peace. Our mind must be stayed on God and we must trust God. Doing one without the other is not listed as a way to achieve perfect peace. Many times our minds are on the Lord, but we doubt Him in our hearts—somehow believing that we know better than He does, or that He is not paying attention, while satan is running amuck with God's head turned.

Other times, we trust God in our heart, but we become idle minded. We become mentally engulfed in the amount of the bills, how troublesome our children are, or how our spouse has hurt us. It is not necessarily that we do not trust God, it is more that we have lost track of Him mentally, emotionally, and usually spiritually.

Focus on God, trust fully in Him, allow God's peace to enter your heart, and watch the difference in that situation. Isaiah did not say that we will not have trials. Neither do we, but you can have God's perfect peace in the midst of them.

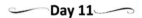Day 11

We Need More Patience

2 My brethren, count it all joy when you fall into various trials, 3 knowing that the testing of your faith produces patience. 4 But let patience have its perfect work, that you may be perfect and complete, lacking nothing.
James 1:2-4

This life is an exercise in faith building. We are instructed that we will, undoubtedly, fall into many different types of temptations. The temptation to sin is of course at the top of the list, but it can take many forms. It can come in the form of wanting to lie to your boss, cheating on a spouse, stealing money from a company, being indifferent to a bum on the street, doubting God, and many other things. I realize that this will not shock anyone. James' direction to us about these temptations is what is shocking.

We are to count it "all" joy. We are not instructed to become irate, upset, bothered, indignant, or even spiritually mad. We are told to count it "all" joy. If you have never really thought about that, allow it to sink in. The scripture places no qualifier on counting it all joy. It does not say count it joy, once it is over. It does not say count it joy, if you win. It does not say count it joy, if they apologize. It simply tells us to count it "all" joy.

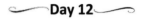 Day 12

We Need More Patience — Part 2

2 My brethren, count it all joy when you fall into various trials, 3 knowing that the testing of your faith produces patience. 4 But let patience have its perfect work, that you may be perfect and complete, lacking nothing.
James 1:2-4

James wants us to know that the trying (testing) of our faith works (builds) patience and that this is why it is joyous, but still to count it "all" joy seems like a lot. However later in the chapter James tells us that enduring temptation will get you the crown of life. Ah ha!

If enduring temptation helps get us to Heaven, is that enough reason to count it "all" joy? This is not to say that we have to enjoy suffering, but it should alter our perceptions and help us realize that our various temptations are working for our good and serve God's purpose in our lives. For that we should count it "all" joy.

List some of the things you must count as "joy."

_____

_____

_____

_____

_____

Day 13

Submit To Who?

21 submitting to one another in the fear of God. 22 Wives, submit to your own husbands, as to the Lord. 23 For the husband is head of the wife, as also Christ is head of the church; and He is the Savior of the body. 24 Therefore, just as the church is subject to Christ, so let the wives be to their own husbands in everything. 25 Husbands, love your wives, just as Christ also loved the church and gave Himself for her, 26 that He might sanctify and cleanse her with the washing of water by the word, 27 that He might present her to Himself a glorious church, not having spot or wrinkle or any such thing, but that she should be holy and without blemish. 28 So husbands ought to love their own wives as their own bodies; he who loves his wife loves himself.
Ephesians 5:21-28

Many Christians are either married or plan on getting married. Many also believe that the union of marriage is being assaulted and undermined, like never before. This is especially troubling because of the importance of marriage to God. God gave the church to Jesus as His bride and Jesus to the church as her husband. Marriage is symbolic, but it is more than that; it is a union that is designed to reflect God's <u>agape</u> love.

A wife's submission to her husband is a sign of commitment to him, but even more so a sign of her commitment to the Lord. After all, it is His commandment to her listed in these scriptures. Think about that. A wife's submission to her husband, is God's Will, not man's. Also, the commandment to husbands to love their wives as Christ loved the church, including a willingness to die for her is directly from God and not just a request from his wife.

Do not overlook the opening line for mutual submission, in "fear" of the Lord. If we do not do it God's way, it is to Him that we will answer. Our treatment of our spouses is an indicator of our love, fear or respect of God. Submission to God means submitting to our spouses. Amen? Amen.

— Day 14 —

How Much Will You Sacrifice to Follow God?

21 Jesus said to him, "If you want to be perfect, go, sell what you have and give to the poor, and you will have treasure in heaven; and come, follow Me." 22 But when the young man heard that saying, he went away sorrowful, for he had great possessions.
Matthew 19:21-22

It is easy to read these scriptures and shake our head at the young man. He approached Jesus asking for the key to eternal life. When Jesus gave it to him, he rejected it. To most of us, it seems like foolishness, but if we are truly honest, how many of us would live out Jesus' commands from that day?

God knows our hearts, so even if we lie to others or ourselves, God already knows whether we would follow Jesus or not. Many of us, just like the rich young ruler, want eternal life. The scripture does not say that the young man was not earnest or sincere when he approached Jesus. As a matter of fact, he told Jesus that he had kept the Ten Commandments since his youth. This indicates that he knew God and was serious about following Him. Yet, when told what it takes to be perfect, he sadly walked away, prompting Jesus to say that the rich would hardly enter Heaven.

We are not suggesting that God has asked many to do what Jesus told the rich young ruler to do, but it is worth considering that if He did, what would be our response. Would we do any better? Would we love God more than our possessions? Would we sacrifice all we have in this world to follow God's Will and receive eternal life? We pray that we all strive to answer yes to those questions.

—— Day 15 ——

Got Faith?

6 But without faith it is impossible to please Him, for he who comes to God must believe that He is, and that He is a rewarder of those who diligently seek Him.

Hebrews 11:6

Faith is one of those highly debatable topics. Is everyone given some? Can you lose it entirely? How much is enough? The questions go on and on, but regardless of the answers, we can be sure that it is impossible to please God without it. Why? Let's consider; can you please a God in which you do not have faith? Will you fear or love a God that you are not sure exists?

Atheists constantly point out that there is not definitive proof that God exists and that may actually be true. If you choose not to believe in God, there may not be anything in existence that can prove that He is real; however, that may be the point. God wants belief in Him to be optional. He wants us to freely choose to believe in him.

Why do you believe?

_____

_____

_____

_____

_____

Day 16

Got Faith? — Part 2

6 But without faith it is impossible to please Him, for he who comes to God must believe that He is, and that He is a rewarder of those who diligently seek Him.
Hebrews 11:6

Think about your answers from Yesterday. If God proves Himself, in such a way, that no one in the world can question or doubt His existence, that is tantamount to taking away our free will. Believing and having faith in God would no longer be a choice to be made.

Faith is the substance of things hoped for the evidence of things not seen. As it is, we are allowed, even encouraged to search for ourselves. We search for meaning. We search for hope. We search for love. We search for God. And for those of us who choose to believe, because we believe and diligently seek Him, God is pleased and we are rewarded for having faith.

Who Sinned?

2 And His disciples asked Him, saying, "Rabbi, who sinned, this man or his parents, that he was born blind?" 3 Jesus answered, "Neither this man nor his parents sinned, but that the works of God should be revealed in him.
John 9:2-3

This may not be a popular sermon topic, but some things happen simply that God may be glorified. How many times have we been like the disciples of Jesus in this scripture? Wondering what we or someone else has done wrong to be put through such trials and tribulations? How many times have we said that someone did not deserve what happened to them?

The works of God are often most evident in the weak, poor, sad, forgotten, and the broken. The least of them is anything but least in the eyes of the Lord. We may be happiest when everything is seemingly going right and there are no evident problems in our lives, but we are most ripe for God to work when we are at our lowest and weakest. When we are weak, He is strong!

<u>All of the inequities in this world are not sin related.</u> Many are, but not all. God is fully capable of planting a circumstance for growth in our lives, whether we think we earned one or not. He is also just as capable of harvesting spiritual fruit from any situation, no matter how terrible it seems. Let us always remember that all things (no matter how unfair they seem) work for the good of those that love the Lord and are called according to His purpose.

Day 18

Glory To God

16 Let your light so shine before men, that they may see your good works and glorify your Father in heaven.
Matthew 5:16

This passage does not suggest that God gave us gifts for our own purposes, but just the opposite. When men see our good works they should glorify our Father which is in Heaven. We often take credit for things when the credit is not truly our own.

If someone comes to us in need of a healing, then God leads us to pray for them, and they get healed; we need to understand that the healing was never ours to give. We were just a vessel God used and He deserves the credit and the glory.

Sharing The Gifts Thaddeus Miles Photography

Day 19

Glory To God — Part 2

16 Let your light so shine before men, that they may see your good works and glorify your Father in heaven.
Matthew 5:16

We should be kind. We should be generous. We should be loving. We should be Godly. But our good works should glorify the God we serve and not ourselves.

With everything that Jesus did and said. How many times did He take personal credit for any of it? He repeatedly told everyone that would listen, that He was simply doing the Will of His Father. He expressly said that the words He spoke were the Words of His Father. He constantly told people about God and the Kingdom of Heaven. Obviously, Jesus is an exceptional example, as God is still receiving glory from the things Jesus did over two thousand years ago. Let us follow His lead and continuously point people toward our Lord.

Day 20

Know Fear/No Fear

1 A Psalm of David. The Lord is my light and my salvation; Whom shall I fear? The Lord is the strength of my life; Of whom shall I be afraid?
Psalm 27:1

Fear wears many faces and has many names. It may be a coming layoff at our jobs, divorce papers being served, or not having enough money to pay the rent. Some people, in other countries, are afraid of losing their lives for practicing their religion. Some fear the abusive parent or spouse they live with. No matter the fear, it is real for the person experiencing it.

The psalmist that wrote this verse feared for his life, but there are people who fear other things, so much that they choose to end their lives rather than face another day. We urge everyone, to respect the crosses that others bear. Everyone's problems are big to them and we all need God to make it through.

⸺ Day 21 ⸺

Know Fear/No Fear — Part 2

1 A Psalm of David. The Lord is my light and my salvation; Whom shall I fear? The Lord is the strength of my life; Of whom shall I be afraid?
Psalm 27:1

What we all have in common is that no matter the fear—the Lord is our light, our salvation, and our strength. He shines in the dark recesses of our lives. He pulls us to safety when we are drowning in doubt and pity. He strengthens us to keep moving when we are stuck in a mess. It is because of Him that we can overcome fear and truly be afraid of nothing and no one. No circumstance, situation, person or people are greater than God. Let us stand strong on who He is and what He has promised!

⸺ Day 22 ⸺

Know Better Do Better

17 Therefore, to him who knows to do good and does not do it, to him it is sin.
James 4:17

It has been said that Christianity is not a religion. It is, instead, a relationship with God. The purpose and title of this book bears witness to that statement. We can strengthen our walk only because our God is a living knowable God, that wants to have a relationship with us. We do our part by accepting His existence and His offering of salvation through Jesus Christ.

However, all relationships are a process. They have lives. They are born, grow, mature, evolve, and change many times over, as the people in them do the same. Though God is always the same, we change and so does our relationship with the Lord.

Day 23

Know Better Do Better — Part 2

> 17 Therefore, to him who knows to do good and does not do it, to him it is sin.
> James 4:17

Hopefully, we are constantly learning more and more about God. He reveals things in His time; as He thinks we are ready, and we progress. First, we learn that there is a God. Second, we learn who He is and what He is. We learn how He feels about us and we learn what He wants from us.

The process will continue as long as we live, but at every point along the way, He expects us to put into practice what we learn. He does not give us everything at once, as we would probably not be able to handle it, but He uncovers it all layer by layer, detail by detail and allows us to practice.

How will you practice today?

_____

_____

_____
_____
_____

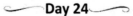 Day 24

Know Better Do Better, Part 3

> 17 Therefore, to him who knows to do good and does
> not do it, to him it is sin.
> James 4:17

Everyone's life experiences are different. While one person works on patience, someone else may be working on peace. One person may be receiving teaching on grace and someone else on mercy. Regardless of what we are learning right now, or what lessons we have picked up in the past, if we are not living them out, it is <u>sin</u>. Knowing what is good in God's sight, and not doing it—is explicitly sin. Learning about God is a wonderful thing, but it comes with responsibility. May we walk in all that we know pleases God today. Amen.

Psalm 4:1
Thaddeus Miles Photography

Day 25

The Gift of Life

23 For the wages of sin is death, but the gift of God is eternal life in Christ Jesus our Lord.
Romans 6:23

If any of us were ever asked to work (do real work) for any large amount of time without receiving a paycheck, we would not be happy. Now imagine being told that your wages for years of work would NEVER be paid to you. Instead, there would be a one-time gift, completely replacing the wages withheld. This is another one of those scenarios that only make sense from a spiritual perspective.

That is exactly what God has done and we are blessed! The wages of the sin that we commit in this world is death. Not earthly death, for we can be alive and dead at the same time; here death means eternal separation from God. We have already earned it, through years of hard work and it would be coming even more surely than the sun rising in the east, but we serve a merciful, gracious and loving God.

He sacrificed His only begotten son Jesus Christ to save us. Now in place of eternal separation from God we can receive a gift. Not just any gift, but an eternal gift. We can live forever in the presence of the Lord in Heaven! Sometimes, I think that we are just not grateful enough for the gift that God has made available to us! We pray that we all appreciate and accept God's grace and mercy.

Day 26

Amen?

14 Let the words of my mouth and the meditation of my heart Be acceptable in Your sight, O Lord, my strength and my Redeemer.
Psalm 19:14

Amen? Yes, this day starts by saying, "So let it be" in response to reading this scripture. We will not go into or ask how often our words and our hearts are not acceptable in the Lord's sight. Today, we will focus on getting it right.

Let us stop, right now, take a deep breath, and thank God for waking us up today. Let us thank Him for all of our blessings from the smallest to the largest we can think of and then, let's thank Him for everything we missed.

It is a day the Lord has made, let us rejoice and be glad in it. Even if we are in the midst of a struggle; bills past due, marriage problems, children misbehaving, jobless, sick/shut-in, car troubles, etc. God is beyond good. God is beyond capable. Let us not lose faith. Let our belief never waver that God loves us. He is our strength and our redeemer. He will not fail us. He will not forget us. Let us keep Him in our heart throughout this day and let His words flow from our lips. Let us glorify Him by the lives we lead on our best days, but also on our most trying. Amen!

Day 27

Where Does It End?

7 The fear of the Lord is the beginning of knowledge,

> But fools despise wisdom and instruction.
> Proverbs 1:7

If fear of the Lord is the "beginning" of knowledge, what is the end? More on that later. If we polled you by a show of hands, "who has been foolish," how many would be honest? We should have all raised our hands.

Let's take today to acknowledge that we often do not give God the reverence, respect, and frankly the fear that is due to Him. We lead our lives, all too often, oblivious to the fact that we deserve death and hell and that it is only by His grace and mercy that we are alive at all. With that said, it is never too late to learn and to do better.

We should fear the Lord because He is our creator. Our eternal resting place is in His hands, to be decided by His judgement. Pleasing Him should be, not just our number one priority; it should probably be our second and third, as well.

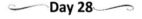Day 28

Where Does It End? — Part 2

> 7 The fear of the Lord is the beginning of knowledge,
> But fools despise wisdom and instruction.
> Proverbs 1:7

We know that devils believe in God and tremble (James 2:19). They seemingly have the "beginning" of knowledge (fear of God). However, fear is obviously not enough to make you serve God or else the devils would not have rebelled and continue to do so.

If fear of God is the beginning, perhaps love of God is the end of knowledge. The more we learn about Him, the more we love Him; especially because He first loved us. The more we love Him, the more we serve Him or at least that is our thought. Let us love God even more than we fear Him and embrace His wisdom and instruction.

How can you love God more?

_____

_____

_____

_____

_____

Day 29

Give And It Shall Be Given

38 Give, and it will be given to you: good measure, pressed down, shaken together, and running over will be put into your bosom. For with the same measure that you use, it will be measured back to you.
Luke 6:38

Many of us have heard this scripture recited in church, at revivals, and on television. If we give, it will be given unto us, until we do not have enough room for it all. It sounds simple enough and it is usually met with hallelujahs and amens. The only people that are usually hesitant to join in with the shouts and praises are those who do not have anything to give or those who just think it sounds too good to be true.

We would like to tell you that those who shout, sing, and dance about this scripture are right to do so. We would also like to tell those that are in the latter group—it is not too good to be true and that you are never too poor to have access to this scripture's blessings. The beauty of this scripture is revealed when read in full context.

— Day 30 —

Give And It Shall Be Given — Part 2

38 Give, and it will be given to you: good measure, pressed down, shaken together, and running over will be put into your bosom. For with the same measure that you use, it will be measured back to you.
Luke 6:38

Jesus was not speaking about money or material things when He made this statement. Luke 6:37 RSV reads, *Judge not, and ye shall not be judged: condemn not, and ye shall not be condemned: forgive, and ye shall be forgiven.*

Notice the semi-colon (;)? Verses 37 and 38 are part of one sentence, meant to be taken and applied together, not separately. If we forgive and avoid judgement and condemnation of others then we will receive, in excess, those same things for ourselves. We can do this even if we are broke. Ultimately, forgiveness will be far more valuable than any worldly goods, so let us shout hallelujah, and forgive as much as we can!

— Day 31 —

Check Your Thankfulness

18 in everything give thanks; for this is the will of God in Christ Jesus for you.
1 Thessalonians 5:18

Looking at the calendar, it won't be long before the holiday season ensues. We were having a discussion with the kids, about why people are so thankful around the holidays and so ungrateful the rest of the year. Some folks are constantly complaining and focusing on what they don't have, rather than being thankful for what they do. The moral of the story is even though man set aside certain days, God ordained everyday as a day of thanks and we have so much to be thankful for!

Your hope should never be that God gives you everything you want. Instead, your hope should always be that you do everything God wants, while trusting that what He gives is what you need.

September
By: Teresa McKellar

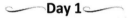 **Day 1**

Pour Out Your Heart

6 Be anxious for nothing, but in everything by prayer and supplication, with thanksgiving, let your requests be made known to God; 7 and the peace of God, which surpasses all understanding, will guard your hearts and minds through Christ Jesus.
Philippians 4:6-7

Pray this today: *Heavenly Father, forgive me for worrying when you have commanded me not to worry. Help me to keep focused on You and Your Word. Keep my heart, mind, and thoughts on You. I thank You for a wonderful day. New mercies are always great! I praise you for taking me through another day and I can't wait to see what You have planned for me today, in Jesus' name, Amen.*

 **Day 2**

Love of the Lord

15 that whoever believes in Him should not perish but[a] have eternal life. 16 For God so loved the world that He gave His only begotten Son, that whoever believes in Him should not perish but have everlasting life.
John 3:15-16

Pray this today: *Thank You Heavenly Father for yet another day; for loving me enough to send Your Son, Jesus Christ, to die for me on the cross. Jesus you are the only person I know that has all the riches in the world but chose to live poor for love's sake. Help me to love as you love. I pray for Godly wisdom,* *strength, and knowledge to continue this race, in Jesus' name, Amen.*

Show God some love.

_____

_____

_____

_____

_____

_____

_____

_____

_____

_____

_____

_____

_____

_____

_____

_____

_____

_____

_____

_____

_____

_____

_____

_____

_____

_____

_____

_____

_____

_____

_____

Day 3

Seeking the Face of the Lord

8 When You said, "Seek My face," My heart said to You,
"Your face, Lord, I will seek."
Psalm 27:8

Early this morning as I sought God's face, I heard the birds singing outside. As the time was ticking away on the clock above my head, vehicles were scurrying to and fro on the highway outside my window. Each was doing what was needed to make it through their day. My day had to begin with prayer.

Pray this today: *As for me, I need you Jesus! Every hour, every minute, every second I need You to survive. Thank you for trading Your life for mine so that I could live eternally, in Jesus' name, Amen.*

Day 4

I Surrender

20 I have been crucified with Christ; it is no longer I who live, but Christ lives in me; and the *life* which I now live in the flesh I live by faith in the Son of God, who loved me and gave Himself for me.
Galatians 2:20

The Heavenly Father knew which child He would call His own, even before birth. He adopted us knowing what we would do; who we would become, even what we would continue to do, but He loves us still. His love for us is amazing. His grace and mercy for us is awesome.

I am excited that He opens up blinded eyes to <u>see</u> His truth, and pierced hearts to <u>accept</u> His truth. His Word changs hearts, and keeps on changing hearts; from the inside out. For this I am grateful and He is worthy of all Praise. Hallelujah!

— Day 5 —

Righteous in Anger

26 "Be angry, and do not sin":[a] do not let the sun go down on your wrath,
Ephesians 4:26

Today we should ask the Lord Jesus, to help us to be mindful of the devices that satan uses to get us to lose hope, of our ability to perceive and our perception to know what we are doing. We want to be obedient to the Lord, with all of our heart.

Don't get angry today; allow righteous anger to translate into action immediately. Everyone gets angry, but allow your anger to be a righteous anger concerning others. We should thank God for tearing down pieces of us to make us more like Him. Ask Him to help you to keep your "right" eye, according to Samuel 11: 1-5.

— Day 6 —

From the Heart Forgive

10 Create in me a clean heart, O God, And renew a steadfast spirit within me.
Psalms 51:10

Thank God that His mercies are new every day that you live. Ask that He forgive you of your sins; known and unknown. Ask the

Lord to help you to keep your hope in Him. Proverbs 13:12 tells me that *Hope deferred makes the heart sick. But when the desire comes, it is a tree of life.* All your hope should be in Him. No matter the circumstances, remember that He controls everything for His glory. In I Thessalonians 5:17, He tells us to *pray without ceasing.*

Pray this today: *Lord allow my mind and spirit to continuously pray for those in leadership all over the world, pray for peace in Jerusalem, and I pray that people would humble themselves, repent, and turn from their wicked ways. Help me to remember that sin will be punished and You will judge the hearts of all men, in Jesus' name, Amen.*

Day 7

Servant of the Lord

21 His lord said to him, 'Well *done,* good and faithful servant; you were faithful over a few things, I will make you ruler over many things. Enter into the joy of your lord.'

Matthew 25:21

Pray this today: *Lord Jesus, thank You for this opportunity to read your Word. I thank You that the Holy Spirit reveals all things as I read Your truth. I am very grateful to be chosen to do Your Will. You are so merciful and Your mercies are new every day. Please continue to guide me, continue to break away the clay on my heart that may cause me to stumble. Clip my wings so that I can soar like eagles. Allow the Holy Spirit to blow wind to guide me in the directions You would have me to go and not my own way. Fill me where I am empty; tear down any wall that is not of You. Rebuild a firm foundation, let me stand on Your Word as a new creation; clean, washed by You, ready to do Your will, to live Holy before You. And when it is time to come home, may my ears hear from You, that I was a good and faithful servant, in Jesus' name, Amen.*

Contemplating the Message
Thaddeus Miles Photography

Day 8

The Price Paid

19 Or do you not know that your body is the temple of the Holy Spirit *who is* in you, whom you have from God, and you are not your own? 20 For you were bought at a price; therefore glorify God in your body and in your spirit,which are God's.

1 Corinthians 6:19-20

You are not your own. You have been bought with a price, chosen by our Father in Heaven, bought by the His Son Jesus Christ and Sealed by the Holy Spirit. Thank God for your change!

Day 9

Spiritual Battle

12 For we do not wrestle against flesh and blood, but against principalities, against powers, against the rulers of the darkness of this age against spiritual *hosts* of wickedness in the heavenly *places*.
Ephesians 6:12

Thank the Heavenly Father for having satan on a leash to roam only where He allows him to roam. Even when you feel like your life is being turned upside down and there is no end to the trials and tribulations—know that God is in control.

Day 10

Give it to God/Relinquish Control

22 Cast your burden on the Lord, And He shall sustain you; He shall never permit the righteous to be moved.
Psalms 55:22

Pray this today: *God in Heaven, please allow me to be still in Your Presence. To wrap myself in the Glory of Your love; to hear Your voice as you speak to my heart. Allow me to crumble before You, to let go of everything I control and give it all to You Lord. Without You Father God, I am nothing; so weak, so fragile, so alone. Nothing manifested is complete without You, in Jesus' name, Amen.*

Broken
things can become
blessed things
if you let God
do the mending.

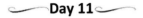 **Day 11**

Repentance for the Love of God

15 For thus says the High and Lofty One Who inhabits eternity, whose name *is* Holy:"I dwell in the high and holy *place, With* him *who* has a contrite and humble spirit,To revive the spirit of the humble, And to revive the heart of the contrite ones.
Isaiah 57:15

Today, thank God for sending His only begotten Son Jesus, to die for our sins. Praise Him that weI can come to Him with a repentant heart and turn our backs on our wicked ways.

Pray this today: *Father God, I am grateful that You have allowed me to live in an area where I can freely read Your Word and worship You openly. I am grateful that You have picked me to be on Your team. Give me Your strength and Wisdom to endure this race! In the name of Jesus, Amen.*

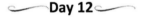 **Day 12**

Heavenly Hope

23 Search me, O God, and know my heart; Try me, and know my anxieties; 24 And see if *there is any* wicked way in me, And lead me in the way everlasting.
Psalms 139:23-24

Pray this today: *You have searched my heart and thoughts for sin and have pointed them out to me, so I may repent and be forgiven. Your thoughts toward me are always for the best and for Your glory. Help me to keep my hope on Heavenly things so that I may walk in Your way forever, in Jesus' name, Amen.*

Day 13

Pray with a Purpose

16 Let us therefore come boldly to the throne of grace, that we may obtain mercy and find grace to help in time of need.
Hebrews 4:16

As I pray and read God's Word, I am reminded that in my prayer life I need to be specific. Not the "Polly-want-a cracker" prayer that goes something like *God bless everybody; help everybody, and be with everybody.* Be reminded to be specific as you bring your prayers to Him.

Pray this today: *I need to be thankful that You have invited me into Your presence, that the Blood of Jesus has provided me a way to access You at any time and that You hear and answer my prayers. Whether You say yes, no or wait, in Jesus' name, Amen.*

Day 14

Sow to Reap the Spiritual

7 Do not be deceived, God is not mocked; for whatever a man sows, that he will also reap. 8 For he who sows to his flesh will of the flesh reap corruption, but he who sows to the Spirit will of the Spirit reap everlasting life. 9 And let us not grow weary while doing good, for in due season we shall reap if we do not lose heart. 10 Therefore, as we have opportunity, let us do good to all, especially to those who are of the household of faith.
Galatians 6:7-10

I remember growing up on a farm and each year there was a time to plant certain vegetables in the garden. I pondered how my Father knew when to plant the corn, the green beans, the potatoes, and so on. I came to one conclusion: my father knew because he had experience in farming to reap the best results.

I began to look at my life as a Christian. There are two places to sow my seed; to the flesh or to the spirit. Where I sow will be the result of what I reap. If I sow to the flesh, I reap fleshy things, such as corruption, but if I sow to my spirit, then I reap Spiritual things, such as everlasting life. Best of all, I have been left an experienced Comforter called the Holy Spirit to help me; an awesome Shepherd to toss the seeds (the Word verse by verse). He gave me amazing Brothers and Sisters to encourage me along the way, shepherds in the best fellowship, and He pervades my Praise and Worship. Remember God doesn't need our praise but we do need to Praise God, and He has allowed this day and any other day, that you still have His breath in your lungs. Want to see a miracle? Look in the mirror! *Amen!*

Day 15

Sparing an Agag

6 For the Lord knows the way of the righteous, But the way of the ungodly shall perish.
Psalms 1:6

In the study of I Samuel, we came across the reading regarding Agag. I began to wonder was there an Agag in my own life? Something that needed to be hacked to pieces, so that it will not come back to stop me from doing God's Will?

Pray this today: *Heavenly Father, I pray that Your Holy Spirit will help me to hack away at the part of my life that needs to be put to death, in Jesus' name, Amen.*

List your Agag's.

_____

_____

_____

_____

_____

_____

_____

_____

Day 16

Spiritual Convictions

3 You will keep *him* in perfect peace, *Whose* mind *is* stayed *on You,* Because he trusts in You.
Isaiah 26:3

Pray this today: *Heavenly Father, allow your Holy Spirit to convict me of anything that is not Your Will. Keep my eyes on You. You are the author and finisher of who I am and who I will become. Keep my mind on Your Word. Allow my heart to receive and accept it, my soul to love it, my spirit to live it and my mind to remember it. Teach my ears to hear Your voice and allow my feet to walk out what Your Holy Spirit is teaching me.*

Give me the desire, courage, and wisdom to obey. Show me one thing that I can do today according to Your will, to meet a need or lift a burden, in Jesus' name, Amen.

Day 17

Holy Spirit Intercedes

26 Likewise the Spirit also helps in our weaknesses. For we do not know what we should pray for as we ought, but the Spirit Himself makes intercession for us with groaning's which cannot be uttered.
Romans 8:26

Pray this today: *Help me to listen to Holy Spirit, whose job is to point me to Jesus. Without your Comforter speaking to my Spirit; I would be lost. I thank you that He intercedes on my behalf daily, in Jesus' name, Amen.*

Day 18

Perfect Example

40 A disciple is not above his teacher, but everyone who is perfectly trained will be like his teacher.
Luke 6:40

There are days that I am trying to be something I am surely not, when I try to show others their wrongs. The Holy Spirit is clearly not what God *hath* created me to be.

Pray this today: *Forgive me Father. If I can't win others to You with a Word, help me to win them with a wordless sermon: let me live it out with my life.*

It is not about me! Let me remember that I am here to spread the Word to men, and the Holy Spirit brings men to Christ, in Jesus' name, Amen.

Day 19

Grace and Mercy

7 He stores up sound wisdom for the upright; *He is* a shield to those who walk uprightly;
Proverbs 2:7

Pray this today: *Thank You for Your Mercy and Grace on this day and for helping me not to abuse either one. As I go through this day, give me Godly Wisdom that is timely, provides protection, gives direction and gives discernment, in Jesus' name, Amen.*

Day 20

Be Committed

30 And you shall love the Lord your God with all your heart, with all your soul, with all your mind, and with all your strength.' This *is* the first commandment.
Mark 12:30

Lack of commitment to the Father will cause you to leave the good path and walk in the ways of darkness. He will help you to be committed to the life change that He has given you. He will allow you to be careful of who you hang out with; they may cause you to stumble. He will allow you to be the "salt" to them, and the light that He has placed in you will outshine the ways of darkness.

Day 21

Trust in the Lord

5 Trust in the Lord with all your heart, And lean not on your own understanding;
Proverbs 3:5

Pray this today: *When you strip everything that I have learned to lean on so that I can lean only on You, I know that I am in a place of "Sanctified Loneliness." Help me to be still, wait on You and get to my "Back Side of the Desert," in Jesus' name, Amen.*

Day 22

Bearing the Burdens of Others

2 Let each of us please *his* neighbor for *his* good, leading to edification. 3 For even Christ did not please Himself; but as it is written, "The reproaches of those who reproached You fell on Me."
Romans 15:2-3

Being strong means being mature, but being weak means being immature. We are not here to please ourselves; in a world that is all about self. The Word tells us that it is not about me, despite what I may think. The Holy Spirit will help us to remember the principle of this Christian life is to please God and not myself. That means, under the right circumstances, pleasing others.

Bear one another's burdens, and so fulfill the law of Christ.
Galatians 6:2

Day 23

Safety in His Presence

91 He who dwells in the secret place of the Most High. Shall abide under the shadow of the Almighty.
Psalms 91:1

Pray this today: *Keep my eyes focused on You; as You are the lifter of my head. I have only one place to look, and that's unto You Lord. Hear my cry and allow me to rest in You and be still. Give me courage; with You, it's ok to be broken. I know the enemy has been defeated and I have been delivered and I am blessed, in Jesus' name, Amen.*

Day 24

Less Love for the Worldly

16 For all that *is* in the world—the lust of the flesh, the lust of the eyes, and the pride of life—is not of the Father but is of the world.
1 John 2:16

Pray this today: *Thank You Lord for <u>not</u> blessing my mess. Sometimes, I want something so badly that I mistake my desires for Your Will. Help me to focus on Your Word, Your Will and Your Way, in Jesus' name, Amen.*

Be transparent. What mess have you been wanting, praying or hoping for God to bless?

_____

_____

_____

_____

_____

Day 25

Well Done

21 His lord said to him, 'Well *done,* good and faithful servant; you were faithful over a few things, I will make you ruler over many things. Enter into the joy of your lord.'
Matthew 25:21

Pray this today: *Lord You are awesome, and what an honor it is to be in Your Presence again. You are amazing to me; how you changed my life, a life once doomed to hell. You washed all of my sins as white as snow. Praise You Lord! Hallelujah! You love me so much. You died and rose again to intercede in prayer for me before Your Father. You prepared a mansion for me in Heaven. One day I know that You are coming back to take me home. Help me to keep my mind on Heavenly things and my heart fully rooted in Your Word. Continue to allow Your Holy Spirit to teach me so that I may glorify You. Let my life be an example and that when I am in Your presence, You will say, "well done my good and faithful servant," in Jesus' name, Amen.*

Day 26

Secure in Knowing

3 Blessed *be* the God and Father of our Lord Jesus Christ, who has blessed us with every spiritual blessing in the heavenly *places* in Christ,
Ephesians 1:3

Pray this today: *Lord I thank you for new mercies, peace, joy and most of all grace. Lord I am nothing without you. Break every chain that is holding me back from giving you 100%. You supply my every need and feed my hungry soul. You are the source of all of my blessings. Pour more of You into me as I give more of me to the Holy Spirit. I love you Lord; You heard my cry. You were there in my darkest hour and You are here with me now. You have never left me, even when I turned my back on You. Forgive me Lord. In the name of Jesus, Amen.*

Day 27

The Lord is My Refuge

2 My soul longs, yes, even faints for the courts of the LORD;
My heart and my flesh cry out for the living God.
Psalms 84:2

The Lord is my Shepherd; I shall not want. My soul longs, even faints for the Lord; my heart and my flesh cry out for the living God. For one day in Your courts is better than a thousand. I would rather be a doorkeeper in the house of my God than dwell in the tents of wickedness. For the Lord God is a sword and shield. The Lord will give grace and glory; no good thing will He withhold from those who walk uprightly.

Power of Reflection — Thaddeus Miles Photography

Day 28

I Am

10 and you are complete in Him, who is the head of all principality and power.
Colossians 2:10

Who am I? I am chosen by God (Ephesians 1:4); I am adopted by God (Ephesians 1:5); I am a child of God (1 John 3:1); I am forgiven by God. (1 John 1:9); I am reconciled by God in harmony with Him (Romans 5:10); I am seen by God as holy, blameless, and above reproach (Colossians 1:21-22); I am sealed with God's Holy Spirit (Ephesians 1:13); I am called to accomplish God's purpose (Romans 8:28,30); I am a full citizen among God's people (Ephesians 2:19); I am justified and declared right in God's sight. (Romans 5:1); I am sanctified and set apart by His Spirit. (I Corinthians 6:11); I am redeemed and bought with Jesus' blood. (Ephesians 1:7); I am cleansed by Jesus' blood for all my sins. (I John 1:7); I am an heir of God and a joint heir with Jesus. (Romans 8:16-17); I am complete in Jesus. (Colossians 2:10); I am an ambassador for Jesus. (II Corinthians 5:20); I am being conformed to the character of Jesus. (Romans 8:29)

Pray this today: *Thank you Lord for giving me worth and letting me see I have a purpose for Your kingdom, in Jesus' name, Amen.*

Day 29

Lords Blessings

22 The blessing of the Lord makes *one* rich, And He adds no sorrow with it.
Proverbs 10:22

Pray this today: *It is a blessing to seek Your face early in the morning while I still can. Please Dear Lord, open my spiritually blinded eyes to see what You are doing in my life and in the lives of my friends and family. You are in control and where ever I think I am in control, let me quickly give it all to You. Help me to keep my eyes on you and my heart deep in You. Keep me abiding in You that I might bear fruit. Thank You for my testimony. Thank You for saving me. Thank You for choosing me to be on Your team. Lord I love You and I am falling more and more in love with you each and every day. You are the best Father I could ever have in my life. You are gracious, merciful and loving. Thank You for turning this heart of stone into a heart of love and compassion, in Jesus' name, Amen.*

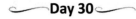**Day 30**

God Our Refuge; Our Strength

10 Be still, and know that I *am* God; I will be exalted among the nations, I will be exalted in the earth!
Psalms 46:10

Pray this today: *Heavenly Father, teach me to be still so I can experience Your eternal Love, when in Your presence. I need you and the certainty of Your Presence when I am going through my storms. Keep my heart and mind focused on You. I am still learning that the ultimate protection against sinking in the midst of my storms is devoting time to develop my friendship and relationship with You, by reading Your Word, praying and being obedient to Your will and Your way, in Jesus' name, Amen.*

October

By: Cynthia Perkins,
Nicole Peeples, Carla Gaskins &
Shayla Donaldson

Day 1

Prayer For The Month
By: Carla Gaskins

The lord is my shepherd I shall not want...
Psalm 23

Pray this today: *Father, in the name of Jesus. I thank you for this day. I thank you for establishing me in this month. I come before you seeking you in advance for the next 30 days. May your hand be upon my life, family, business, health and the vision that you have given me. I thank you in advance for the manifestation of your promises. I bring everything and lay it all at your feet. I come before the throne of grace seeking you today for forgiveness. I repent for all wrong doing, any sinful act against you, I ask my Heavenly Father that you forgive me. I pray God that the presence of your Holy Spirit will rest upon me. Dispatch your angels to cover and protect me from harm and danger. I bind the hand of the enemy and superimpose the Blood of Jesus over every plan and attack over my life, my family, finances, business and my education. I thank you God in advance for the manifestation of all your promises for the month. I thank you Father, in Jesus' name Amen.*

Day 2

An Uncommon Response
By: Cynthia Perkins

15 Also the word of the Lord came to me, saying, 16 "Son of man, behold, I take away from you the desire of your eyes with one stroke; yet you shall neither mourn nor weep, nor shall your tears run down. 17 Sigh in silence, make no mourning for the dead; bind your turban on your

head, and put your sandals on your feet; do not cover
your lips, and do not eat man's bread of sorrow."
Ezekiel 24:15-17

For greater clarity, you may read through the 27th verse. God tells Ezekiel that He is going to take his wife, knowing that she is precious to the man of God. When it takes place, Ezekiel does as he has been instructed by God and the people do not understand his reaction. So they ask for a sign as to why he does not respond to the usual customs of their culture.

God has a plan for each of our lives. Because He devised the plan, we do not know the specifics of how to reach the destination. Yet, because we belong to Him, He expects us to trust Him for our comfort and provision. This is not easy to accomplish; as our "flesh" may lead us into our own way of thinking and to our own understanding. Much like Ezekiel, we must always be diligent and steadfast believing upon His Promises and His Word. In the tribulation, it may seem as if we will perish, but where there is destruction, there is restoration for those who love the LORD. Our God will never forsake us nor will He leave us without provision or His comfort. And no matter how difficult it may seem, we will survive, sometimes surpassing expectations with an uncommon response.

— Day 3 —

Patience A Thousand Fold
By: Nicole Peeples

9 The Lord is not slack concerning His promise, as some count slackness, but is longsuffering toward us, not willing that any should perish but that all should come to repentance. 10 But the day of the Lord will come as a thief in the night, in which the heavens will pass away with a great noise, and the

elements will melt with fervent heat; both the earth and the works that are in it will be burned up.

2 Peter 3:9-10

The preceding verse talks about how a thousand years is as one day for God. I was thinking about how we always talk about being patient and waiting for God's timing. In a world, skewed toward "immediate gratification," we hate to wait. I admit, I would rather microwave my food, than wait for it to warm in the oven. Honestly, it tastes better when you warm it the old-fashioned way.

But today, I was thinking about just how patient God is toward us. We fail Him many times, and in many ways. He teaches us lessons, repeatedly, and we keep failing the tests. Are we in the slow class or what?! Why don't we learn that if He made a way for us once that He is capable of making a way again! Predictably, we don't! We cry, complain, stress, and become aggravated when we have to wait! But, He waits on us, patiently while we have temper-tantrums; and does it lovingly.

Are you this patient with your loved ones? Could you ever be?

_____
_____
_____
_____
_____

Day 4

Patience A Thousand Fold — Part 2
By: Nicole Peeples

9 The Lord is not slack concerning His promise, as some count slackness, but is longsuffering toward us, not willing that any

should perish but that all should come to repentance. 10 But the day of the Lord will come as a thief in the night, in which the heavens will pass away with a great noise, and the elements will melt with fervent heat; both the earth and the works that are in it will be burned up.

2 Peter 3:9-10

As a teacher, my pet-peeve is when I have audibly said the page number to the book we are reading, I have written it on the board, and repeated it again, and then someone in the class asks me, "what page is it on?" I think to myself, "Are you kidding me? Do you not see it on the board? Did you not hear me when I said it two times?" However, as sad as it is, I think I do the same thing to God. Did I not read the solution to my problem in the Word? Did He not speak it to me through a prophecy? Did He not give me an assurance in my Spirit? (Revelation: I must be more patient with the students because I do the same thing to God!)

Today, reflect on just how patient God is toward you and reciprocate that same fruit of the Spirit to Him! By the way, you can find that in 2 Peter 3:15. Bear in mind that our Lord's patience means salvation.

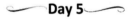 **Day 5**

The Spirit Of Offense
By: Nicole Peeples

28 Come to Me, all you who labor and are heavy laden, and I will give you rest. 29 Take My yoke upon you and learn from Me, for I am gentle and lowly in heart, and you will find rest for your souls. 30 For My yoke is easy and My burden is light.

Matthew 11:28-30

I recently read a devotional by Jennifer LeClaire. I meditated deeply on it; consider this Spirit-inspired wisdom. When the feeling of hurt arises, the spirit of offense arises to fortify the pain, tempting you to hold on to the grudge in your heart. Therefore, the proper response to emotional pain of the soul is always an immediate confession of forgiveness from the heart. The alternative to forgiveness from the heart is the ongoing torment of the soul. So, if you want to be free from your hurts and wounds, take thoughts of forgiveness, meditate on them and confess them rather than taking thoughts of the hurt, meditating on them and confessing them. This is God's way— and it's the only way that brings true healing. Also, while you are at it, pray for those who have hurt you. This process will cleanse your heart and renew your mind. And you will walk free from the pain of your past.

 Day 6

Cover Your Seed
By: Nicole Peeples

17 So then faith comes by hearing, and hearing by the word of God.
Romans 10:17

It is vitally important to speak positive words in your home, over your life, and especially <u>to</u> your children. As I was preparing my lesson plans for my students for the approaching school year, I came across this research information that I found astounding. There is a significant difference in the quantity and the quality of words used that varies with socioeconomic levels. In other words, the less money one makes, not only are fewer words used to speak to the children but fewer positive words are used as well. Here's the research information:

In a typical hour, the average child hears:

- Welfare – 616 words with 5 being positive and 11 negative
- Working Class – 1,251 words with 12 being positive and 7 negative
- Professional – 2,153 with 32 being positive and 5 negative

Not to end today on a negative note, but let's end todays devotional here and you write out your thoughts on the statistics above. You may or may not fit into one of these categories. But think about it. We will finish tomorrow.

_____
_____
_____
_____
_____

Day 7

Cover Your Seed — Part 2
By: Nicole Peeples

17 So then faith comes by hearing, and hearing by
the word of God.
Romans 10:17

Wow! That was all I could think to myself when I read those statistics. It is important that we strive to speak positive words over the lives of our seed. There are many scriptures in the Bible that you can use to speak over his or her life, especially when it appears they are far from it! Let them hear you speak it! Faith comes by hearing! They begin to believe what you speak, good or bad! So, why don't you tell them that they are going to college, they will not have children out of wedlock, they will not be a statistic, and they will be successful! The list goes on and on! Try it on yourself too! *So then faith cometh by hearing, and hearing by the word of God!*

Day 8

Do Something With The Word
By: Nicole Peeples

15 He sends out His command to the earth; His word runs very swiftly.
Psalm 147:15

How many times have you heard a life changing Word? If we desire change, we must be active in preparation. We can be extremely excited about a great Word, but make no attempt to actively move from where we are, to where we need to be. EFFORT is required. My questions to you are, what MORE are you making room for and what are you BELIEVING? Truly think about your answer. Now, what steps have you taken this week, to prepare for _____

_____ (Fill in your answer here)!
If the answer is "not much" or "nothing," then can you honestly say that you believe God enough to make room? It could be that God has a multitude of blessings and doors that He wants to open for you, but it starts with taking the first step toward what He already instructed you to do. Hearing the Word should transcend becoming excited, because excitement is temporary. The Word should motivate you to change your perspective about not only God, but even about yourself. Do something with your Word. Make it active in your life!

God's Promise
isn't that He'll keep bad
things from happening; it's that
He'll be there if they do.

Day 9

It Is My Pleasure To Serve You
By: Cynthia Perkins

4 how he went into the house of God, took and ate the showbread, and also gave some to those with him, which is not lawful for any but the priests to eat?" 5 And He said to them, "The Son of Man is also Lord of the Sabbath."
Luke 6: 4-5

Too often we forget, Jesus as a servant, which was His natural state of being as a giver. In such, the lesson of serving others through our actions and the act of being "brotherly" gets lost in our expectation of what we are receiving. To give from our heart means having no expectation to receive anything in return but to be of purpose in meeting the need of someone else. Let us reflect on Jesus as the true "Giver" of life.

_____
_____
_____
_____
_____

Day 10

Whatever He Says, BELIEVE!
By: Nicole Peeples

20 So they rose early in the morning and went out into the Wilderness of Tekoa; and as they went out, Jehoshaphat stood and said, "Hear me, O Judah and you inhabitants of Jerusalem: Believe in the Lord your God, and you shall be established; believe His prophets, and you shall prosper."
2 Chronicles 20:20

This is not the season to be slack in your effort to put in work with your faith; nor is it the season to doubt God. Our disbelief can really have detrimental effects over our lives, including generations to come; let me show you. God told Abraham and Sarah that they would have a child. Some time passed and it had not happened. Sarah decided to help God out and tell Abraham to go with her maid, Hagar. She didn't just get tired of waiting, she didn't believe God enough to continuing waiting for the full promise. Oh, don't point fingers at Sarah, because we do it too. Instead of waiting for the financial release, we go get a loan and end up in worse shape than before; when all we should have done is sow seed, wait, and believe. All Sarah was supposed to do was let Abraham sow seed, wait, and believe!

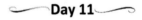Day 11

Whatever He Says, BELIEVE! — Part 2
By: Nicole Peeples

> 20 So they rose early in the morning and went out into the Wilderness of Tekoa; and as they went out, Jehoshaphat stood and said, "Hear me, O Judah and you inhabitants of Jerusalem: Believe in the Lord your God, and you shall be established; believe His prophets, and you shall prosper."
> 2 Chronicles 20:20

As a result, Ishmael was born. He was not the promised child. Conflict ensued between the two baby-mamas and children. And from that day until this day, the descendants of the promised son, Isaac and Ishmael still fight. Yes, the Arabs and the Jews still violently feud among themselves. Both Sarah and Abraham listened to the lesser voice. He listened to her; she listened to the adversary. They both operated in disbelief! Don't mess it up for your season, for your life or for your bloodline. One moment of disbelief, can alter your entire life. But here's the flip side, your unwavering faith in His Word, will cause you to prosper, advance, be profitable, flourish, and finish well. Sounds like success to me!

I Believe! Do you?

_____

_____

_____

_____

_____

_____

_____

_____

_____

Day 12

Don't Make God Question You
By: Nicole Peeples

9 Then the Lord God called to Adam and said
to him, "Where are you?"
Genesis 3:9

This scripture is the only time we read where God questioned Adam's whereabouts. Why? Because he was out of order; out of place, not in his rightful place. All because he had sinned. After God made everything, He called it good. He called it good because He could see His reflection in it. After all, He created us in His image and likeness. So, when Adam broke his fellowship with God, Adam ultimately left his place. Where are you Adam?

Where are we, as the church? Are we in our rightful place operating in the fullness of His image and likeness?

Unfortunately, immediately Adam came up with excuses. And, on top of those excuses, instead of being the protector of Eve, he "threw her under the bus!" He told God that he messed up because of Eve! Being out of place affects everything! When we don't fall in line with our assignment and position, then others must do a job that they may not be ordained or anointed to do. It may get done, but it's not as effective as it should be. So, we all become a little less effective because someone was out of place. There is a clarion call for the family to assume their Godly position, not as the world sees it, but as God has ordained it. It starts with you.

Day 13

The Family Is Under Attack
By: Nicole Peeples

10 The thief does not come except to steal, and to kill, and to destroy. I have come that they may have life, and that they may have it more abundantly.
John 10:10

The devil wants to move us out of the Will of God in every aspect of our lives. It starts with the family unit. There are many threats to the family; things that we have deemed appropriate and normal because it has become the norm through society's standards. However, it was never the way God intended. The enemy's job is to steal, kill, and destroy. Destroy, simply means to put an end to; render useless; give way to eternal misery; take away from the whole. Wow! Sounds like the modern family! Let's look at them individually;

The Cause		The Effect/Result
• Laws have put an end to marriage as	→	Same sex marriages are increasing.

it was designed between man and woman!

• Society is gravitating toward putting an end to marriage altogether.	→	Common law marriages have skyrocketed.
• Popular culture is rendering traditional joining together useless.	→	Far too many folks have been convinced that they don't need a man/woman (a mate).
• People want to avoid eternal misery.	→	Baby mama drama and baby daddy drama is always misery.
• Divorces are taking away from the "whole family."	→	Any dissolution of marriage is taking away from the whole family unit.

None of these things are what God designed! However, the good news is, He has come that we might have life and have it more abundantly! That life is one that is purposeful, full, strong, efficient, active, enjoyable! It can only be achieved through Him.

— Day 14 —

My Stomach Hurts
By: Cynthia Perkins

55 For My flesh is food indeed, and My blood is drink indeed.
56 He who eats My flesh and drinks My blood abides in Me,

and I in him. 57 As the living Father sent Me, and I live because of the Father, so he who feeds on Me will live because of Me. 58 This is the bread which came down from heaven--not as your fathers ate the manna, and are dead. He who eats this bread will live forever.

John 6:55-58

The more I try to eat healthy, the more difficult the task becomes. "It's a lifestyle change; not a diet," is what I've heard. But somehow, I can't seem to stick to the new lifestyle long enough to get past the discomfort of not having the things I should not eat. Even though the old way of eating makes my stomach hurt, I just can't seem to maintain that healthy way of eating! So consequently, the new changes are never permanent.

Likewise, if we don't feed our Spirit with the right types of food daily, our soul will hurt for something that is not achievable through an old or fleshly way of living. Thus, our Spirit does not grow and mature into a Godly way of living and we struggle with allowing the "change" to take effect. A "lifestyle change" takes place due to the presence of the Holy Spirit leading and guiding our lives. Yielding to the Holy Spirit allows the mindset to change and the body to surrender, so that the cohesiveness of "becoming a whole, Spirit-filled being" is permanent.

—— Day 15 ——

The Roar Of A Lion
By: Carla Gaskins

10 They shall walk after the Lord. He will roar like a lion. When He roars, Then His sons shall come trembling from the west;

Hosea 11:10

A lion roars to establish its presence, territory and communication. They mostly roar at night because the air is thinner and sound travels further. A lion's roar can go as far as five miles. I can recall a time I was awakened from my sleep by the sound of a roaring lion. I woke up trembling. However, I felt safe and had a reverential fear at the same time. Immediately, the Holy Spirit caught my attention. I knew God was commanding me to pray. The sound was powerful and loud, as if someone had placed surround sound in my bedroom. I looked over at my husband and he was sound asleep. When you read the Word of God or hear it preached does it cause your spirit to be awakened? Does it cause you to follow Him and commune with Him? Are you allowing the word to be established in your life? Jesus is the Lion of the tribe of Judah in Revelation 5:5. Today as you meditate on the Word of God, listen for the roar of the Lion of the tribe of Judah. He wants to commune with you and establish you. Let the roar of God's word awaken you to attention and follow the leading of His Holy Spirit. Rest in His presence, as in Him is safety!

Do you hear God commanding you to pray?

Day 16

The Prayer For Children
By: Carla Gaskins

13 Then little children were brought to Him that He might put His hands on them and pray, but the disciples rebuked them. 14 But Jesus said, "Let the little children come to Me, and do not forbid them; for of such is the kingdom of heaven." 15 And He laid His hands on them and departed from there.
Matthew 19:13-15

Father in the name of Jesus, I ask that you call the children unto You according to this scripture. No one can hinder them from coming unto You. Give them freedom to worship You as their true and living God. Let no distractions by way of TV, music, social media, technology and magazines, of any kind, destroy their minds. Lay Your heavenly hands upon them in the realm of the spirit and cover them with the Blood of Jesus. While even in their youth, call them to repentance, as in 2nd Peter 3:9. It is Your desire that none should perish. Transform them through Your Holy Spirit. Do not allow them to be unequally yoked in relationships. Keep their thoughts pure, according to Philippians 4:8. Also, when the time is right they will go with You, according to Matthew 28:18-20, in Jesus' name, Amen.

Pray the scriptures within the prayer over your children or the young people in your lives every day.

> *Hear, my son, your father's instruction,*
> *and forsake not your mother's teaching,*
> *for they are a graceful garland for your head*
> *and pendants for your neck.*
>
> (Proverbs 1:8–9 ESV)

Day 17

Stolen Goods
By: Carla Gaskins

8 Again, the devil took Him up on an exceedingly high mountain, and showed Him all the kingdoms of the world and their glory. 9 And he said to Him, "All these things I will give You if You will fall down and worship me." 10 Then Jesus said to him, "Away with you, Satan! For it is written, 'You shall worship the Lord your God, and Him only you shall serve.'"
Matthew 4:8-10

Whatever is done in the natural, so it is in the spirit. When someone gets caught purchasing stolen goods they can be arrested, just like the person that stole the goods. There is a penalty for stealing and receiving. What will it cost you, for taking or accepting those goods? You are jeopardizing your relationship with God. Is that relationship important to you? Why or Why not?

_____

_____

_____

_____

_____

Day 18

Stolen Goods — Part 2
By: Carla Gaskins

8 Again, the devil took Him up on an exceedingly high mountain, and showed Him all the kingdoms of the world and their glory. 9 And he said to Him, "All these things I will give You if You will fall down and worship me." 10 Then Jesus said

to him, "Away with you, Satan! For it is written, 'You shall worship the Lord your God, and Him only you shall serve.'"
Matthew 4:8-10

Are you being tempted by satan? Be careful, he has stolen goods. You will be arrested in the realm of the spirit for receiving stolen goods. God is watching. In Matt 4:8-10, he did the same to Jesus. Satan stole it from the first Adam but Jesus being the second Adam came and took it back. Satan is offering you something Jesus already took back. The reason satan can proposition you with temptation is because he is the ruler of this world. What makes him ruler? People who compromise and live sinful lifestyles. They worship him and give him authority over everything they own. Peace, family, life and so much more. The one you give more attention to is who has your heart. Take back what the enemy stole. Jesus paid the price already. Don't get caught with stolen goods.

Day 19

"Psalm Of Thanksgiving" Prayer
By: Carla Gaskins

34 Oh, give thanks to the Lord, for He is good! For His mercy endures forever.
1 Chronicles 16:34

We *thank You for this day Father. Another day to love life, another opportunity to repent, forgive and serve. Another day of peace and to experience Your promise, to live life and live it more abundantly. We decree and declare that this day will not end without every need being met in Jesus' name.*

Thank You for putting us in families and communities that nurture through the love of Jesus. Thank You for allowing me to see Your love and kindness in those around me; from a smile, a hug and a simple greeting, as they pass by. Thank You that Your eyes are forever upon me. Thank You for the sacrifice of Your Son to extend an opportunity of eternal life with You.

Thank You that I am able to lift my hands in praise unto You. Thank You for being You, the Almighty, all-knowing, amazing and powerful God that You are. Thank You for Your mercy and Your grace, as I am never worthy of it. Thank You Father, in Jesus' name, Amen.

Your child 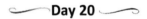. (Add Your name in the blank.)

If you have other things to be thankful for, make certain that you extend the prayer and add those. God never tires of hearing us say thank you and we should never tire of saying it.

⌐⌐⌐Day 20 ⌐⌐

What Are You Wearing?
By: Shayla Donaldson

12 Therefore, as the elect of God, holy and beloved, put on tender mercies, kindness, humility, meekness, longsuffering;
Colossians 3:12

Trying to find what to wear on a daily basis is a dramatic event. I try to plan ahead and think about what outfit I should wear, so I don't stress in the morning. That should work; but I struggle. Partly because I am indecisive and partly because my plans never tend to work out in that area. But I always end up leaving my house looking halfway decent and "put together."

Praise God, I don't have to try to figure out what I should "put on" in the spirit. The Word of God clearly indicates what we as believers should "wear" every day. The NIV version says "clothe yourselves." Think about it like a standard uniform. We, as disciples of Christ, are expected to wear a uniform that displays Godly characteristics. Today, purpose in your heart to wear the Christian uniform. Make a conscious choice to put on the characteristics of love, compassion, kindness, humility and patience. This is how people will know that we belong to Christ.

Day 21

Prayer For Letting Go Of The Past
By: Carla Gaskins

5 I acknowledged my sin to You, And my iniquity I have not hidden. I said, "I will confess my transgressions to the Lord," And You forgave the iniquity of my sin. Selah
Psalm 32:5

Father I realize that I am helpless in saving myself. I glory in what Jesus has done for me. I leave everything and everyone in my past that have hindered me from moving forward in You and the purpose for my life. I put aside all sources of my own confidence, seeing them worth less than nothing, in order that I may experience Jesus and be one with Him. Father I accept Your Son as my Lord and Savior. I have been given the authority, power, privilege and right to become Your child. I put my life in proper perspective. Knowing I have been crucified with Jesus Christ and I no longer live but I live with Christ in me. I live by faith in the Son of God, who loves me first and gave Himself for me.

I trust You Lord with all my heart. I lean not unto my own understanding; in all my ways I will acknowledge You and You alone will lead me on the righteous path. It is through the power of Your resurrection and suffering that I come to know You fully for who You are. I acknowledge that I am not perfect and I haven't learned all I should but I will work toward that day when I finally am what Christ saved me for and want me to be, in Jesus' name. Amen.

─── **Day 22** ───

Be Not Afraid
By: Shayla Donaldson

9 "Have I not commanded you? Be strong and of good courage; do not be afraid, nor be dismayed, for the LORD your God is with you wherever you go."
Joshua 1:9

"I'm too afraid of the unknown to allow God to have His way in my life." This was the beginning of a journal entry that I recently wrote. I was praying about a particular situation and I felt like I kept going back and forth with the Holy Spirit about what to do. I knew what the Spirit was leading me to do but fear and anxiety kept me from fully accepting it. As I was praying, the Spirit asked me a question, "What one thing is holding you back from obeying my instructions?" As I sat there and thought about it for a few minutes, I wrote that statement down as my response. I began to cry. I didn't want to disobey God because of fear. But the truth was I was really terrified about taking this step, because I didn't know what to expect and what the end result would be.

We have read about fear at other times during this year. What are you still afraid of?

_____

_____

_____

_____

_____

~~Day 23~~

Be Not Afraid — Part 2
By: Shayla Donaldson

9 "Have I not commanded you? Be strong and of good courage; do not be afraid, nor be dismayed, for the LORD your God is with you wherever you go."
Joshua 1:9

I was reminded of the story of Peter walking on the water with Jesus, in Matthew 14. When he encountered Jesus, he was unsure if that was really Him but said, "Lord if it is You, command me to come." He then stepped out; just like that. It seemed so easy, until Peter realized that he was actually walking on the water and felt the raging winds. However, Jesus did not let Him sink. In principle, I knew that He wouldn't let me either. But I had to allow my mind to catch up with what my faith already knew.

So I prayed these words: *Lord, You have not given me the spirit of fear. So these feelings of fear and anxiety are not of You. Give me courage to know that You are with me no matter where I must go. Give me the strength to take the first step and most importantly to keep my eyes and ears focused on You, instead of the distractions around me. I want to obey You and I want You to have Your way in my life at all costs. I yield completely to You. I cast out fear and doubt and worry and any other feeling that is not like You. And I call forth peace and love and joy. It is so, in Jesus' Name! Amen!*

Day 24

Prayer For Giving God Glory
By: Carla Gaskins

1 I beseech you therefore, brethren, by the mercies of God, that you present your bodies a living sacrifice, holy, acceptable to God, which is your reasonable service.
Romans 12:1

I acknowledge Your mercy, oh God! I offer my body as a living sacrifice, which is holy and pleasing to You. God this is my worship unto You; it is not by my own strength but it is You, Oh Lord, who is working in me. Giving me power and desire, both to do Your will and work for Your good pleasure, satisfaction and delight. I will never draw back or shrink in fear. I was bought for a price. I will call on You in the day of trouble. I give You honor and glorify You. I rejoice because You delivered me and have given me control and dominion over darkness. You, Father, have transformed me into the kingdom with the love of Your son. I will praise You; I will confess You as my Lord with my whole heart. I will glorify You forever in the name of Jesus. I allow my life to lovingly express, in all things, speaking truth and living in truth through Your word. To You and You alone Father I give glory honor and praise, in Jesus' name, Amen.

Day 25

Don't Count God Out
By: Shayla Donaldson

5 But now, do not therefore be grieved or angry with yourselves because you sold me here; for God sent me

before you to preserve life. 6 For these two years the famine has been in the land, and there are still five years in which there will be neither plowing nor harvesting. 7 And God sent me before you to preserve a posterity for you in the earth, and to save your lives by a great deliverance. 8 So now it was not you who sent me here, but God; and He has made me a father to Pharaoh, and lord of all his house, and a ruler throughout all the land of Egypt.

Genesis 45:5-8

I know you may not want to hear this, because there are days that I certainly don't either, but know this: there is a greater purpose for what you are going through! It may feel like your situation is hopeless but God placed you in this and nothing He does is in vain! Everything He does is with purpose and that purpose is always bigger than us! Our situation, experience or circumstance cannot be contained in our small life. It must be magnified and glorified through Jesus Christ! More often than not, we don't know the significance or lesson of our trials until we come through it! This means we have to trust God and know that with Him we will get through.

Day 26

Don't Count God Out — Part 2
By: Shayla Donaldson

5 But now, do not therefore be grieved or angry with yourselves because you sold me here; for God sent me before you to preserve life. 6 For these two years the famine has been in the land, and there are still five years in which there will be neither plowing nor harvesting. 7 And God sent me before you to preserve a posterity for you in the earth, and to save your lives by a great deliverance. 8 So now it was not you who sent me here, but God; and He

has made me a father to Pharaoh, and lord of all his house, and a ruler throughout all the land of Egypt.
Genesis 45:5-8

If nothing else, I want to encourage you today to KEEP GOING!!!! There is an end and God is keeping you through this season! God is using your experiences to bring out great possibilities! What you experience now may save your entire family or even community later! So don't give credit to the enemy! He could not orchestrate such a great path to your destiny. Only a great and mighty God could create every step, good and bad, even accounting for mishaps, mess ups, and mistakes and still guide you in the right direction to get to your next dimension!

What are some of the areas in which you need encouragement or areas that you need God to work in?

_____
_____
_____
_____
_____

Day 27

"Thy Will Be Done," Prayer For Submission
By: Carla Gaskins

9 In this manner, therefore, pray: Our Father in heaven, Hallowed be Your name. 10 Your kingdom come. Your will be done On earth as it is in heaven.
Matthew 6:9-10

Father, in the name of Jesus, I pray that Your will be done in my life as it is in heaven. I am Your workmanship created in Christ

Jesus. Show me how to do the good work You have ordained for my life; living the life, You pre-ordained for me to live. Teach me Your Will and Your ways. Let Your Holy Spirit lead me into an upright lifestyle.

You gave Yourself for my sins to rescue me and deliver me from the wicked one. I am not conformed to this world but I am transformed by the renewing of my mind, that I may prove what is that good and acceptable and perfect Will of God for my life. You have separated and set apart my life for pure and holy living; that I should know how to possess, control and manage my own body from impurity and profane things.

Father thank You for choosing me, picking me out for Yourself as Your own, before the foundation of the world, that I may be holy and blameless in Your sight. You have predestinated me into the adoption of Your family, Jesus Christ according to the good pleasure of Your will. Father let Your will be done on earth, in my life as it is in heaven, in Jesus' name, Amen.

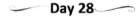 **Day 28**

He Still Loves Me
By: Shayla Donaldson

8 But God demonstrates His own love toward us, in that while we were still sinners, Christ died for us.
Romans 5:8

I was having a conversation with my husband recently and he asked me a simple question, "Have I told you that I love you today?" Well, he hadn't and I wanted to make sure He knew (since he asked). His response was, "Well, you should know I do, whether I tell you or not." I thought about his statement; he was right. Of course I knew he loved me. He demonstrated his love for me every day. I felt his love in the small but meaningful things he would do for me and our kids or the way he would look at me while in conversation. I also felt it by the way he would overlook my selfish dramatics (yes, I have those moments) and forgive my rants. Even if he didn't tell me he demonstrated his love for me by showing me and proving to me, in every possible way, how important I was to him.

Day 29

He Still Loves Me — Part 2
By: Shayla Donaldson

8 But God demonstrates His own love toward us, in that while we were still sinners, Christ died for us.
Romans 5:8

Just as I knew, beyond a shadow of a doubt, that my husband loved me, in this same way, our heavenly Father loves us. He shows us every day He is faithful, by waking us up in our right mind and allowing us to go about our day; sometimes without even giving Him due praise. Yet, He still extends His love and grace and new mercies our way. What is even more remarkable? He demonstrated the greatest act of love before we were even in a position to receive it. He gave His Only Son as a selfless exchange for our sins. If that's not love, I don't know what is!

Day 30

Prayer Of "God's Praise And Magnification"
By: Carla Gaskins

1 ... I will bless the Lord at all times; His praise shall continually be in my mouth. 2 My soul shall make its boast in the Lord;

The humble shall hear of it and be glad. 3 Oh, magnify the Lord with me, And let us exalt His name together. 4 I sought the Lord, and He heard me, And delivered me from all my fears... 6 This poor man cried out, and the Lord heard him, And saved him out of all his troubles. 7 The angel of the Lord encamps all around those who fear Him, And delivers them. 8 Oh, taste and see that the Lord is good; Blessed is the man who trusts in Him! 9 Oh, fear the Lord, you His saints! There is no want to those who fear Him. 10 The young lions lack and suffer hunger; But those who seek the Lord shall not lack any good thing.

Psalm 34: 1- 10

Pray this today: *Father, we speak well of You. We will always praise You with our mouth. Our souls will bless You with excessive satisfaction for who You are. With unity, we will exalt Your name; You are awesome and we shout hallelujah. When we cried out in fear, You heard us and delivered us. We were not ashamed to see You and we found You in Your radiance when we cried out to You; from our troubles You saved us. You Lord are always ever present and we have a reverential fear of You. We perceive You to be good; oh how we trust in You. There is no want for those who fear You. There is no lack when we seek You. You are a God who will never leave us or forsake us! This I pray, In the name of Jesus, Amen.*

Give God the praise that is due to Him. Exhort Him and extol Him today. Meditate on Psalm 34:1-10.

_____
_____
_____
_____
_____
_____
_____

Day 31

Rest in Worship
By: Shayla Donaldson

14 And He said, "My Presence will go with you, and I
will give you rest."
Exodus 33:14

More often than not, I feel tired and overwhelmed. After a long day of work, running errands and then coming home to navigate through parental responsibilities and household duties I am just worn out! And I try my best to use that as an excuse to not spend time with God. "Lord, I'm so tired I'll just read the Scripture in the morning" or "I am so exhausted from such a long day. Let me go to bed now and I'll get up earlier tomorrow and pray." I make these statements in hope that God will excuse me from devotion and quality time with Him. Sometimes I think I feel that spending time with God is another added burden when really it's the best thing I can do to feel less stressed, overwhelmed and tired.

It doesn't make sense to my natural way of thinking but ironically I have learned that when I spend time with Him in worship I feel refreshed, renewed and rejuvenated. The more I worship the less tired and overwhelmed I feel. Try it today! I guarantee that if you invite His presence into your spirit He will give you true rest. It will be better than any sleep you will ever get!

Pray this today. *Lord, have Your way in my schedule today. No matter how busy I think I am or how many things I feel the need to accomplish today let me never forget to invite Your Presence into my agenda. Let me spend time in worship with you so that*

I may find the true meaning of rest and experience a refreshing like never before, in Jesus' name, Amen.

November

By: Tamika and Mark J. Avery &
Adrienne Goodlow

Day 1

Sundown
By: Tamika & Mark J. Avery

26 "Be angry, and do not sin": do not let the sun go down on your wrath, 27 nor give place to the devil.
Ephesians 4:26-27

In January, we are told to leave the junk in the previous year. We must do that on a daily basis because little vestiges of emotions carry over from day to day. One of those stubborn little foxes is anger. When the sun set yesterday, you should have made an effort to leave all your anger in the previous day.

Have you ever been cut off in traffic? Treated unfairly at a job? Ostracized by family members? Hurt by your children? Betrayed by friends? Whether we have experienced one or all, we have all been angry. It is an unavoidable emotion. However, *how* we deal with it, as Christians, is very important.

James 1:20 says, *for the wrath of man does not produce the righteousness of God.* This verse connects anger to sin and sin to giving the devil place in our lives. We will not deceive anyone into believing that anger is avoidable. It is not, but to sin because of it is a choice. Also, to remain angry; to make the decision to hold onto anger is to give place to the devil.

Day 2

Sundown — Part 2
By: Tamika & Mark J. Avery

26 "Be angry, and do not sin": do not let the sun go down on your wrath, 27 nor give place to the devil.
Ephesians 4:26-27

Letting go of anger, admittedly, can be difficult. Depending on who experiences it and how it happens, anger can very easily be overwhelming and spiral into depression and hate. This scripture gives us advice on how to keep that from happening. It does not say, "Do not get angry." It does say do not let the sun go down on your wrath. As Christians we must be diligent in dealing with our anger and wrath quickly and in a Godly manner; while avoiding sin and allowing God's love to reign in our hearts, instead of hate and the devil.   The sun is going down somewhere, let go of anger before it sets.

How has anger been masquerading in your life? What do you need to let go before sundown?

_____

_____

_____

_____

_____

Day 3

Maturity
By: Tamika & Mark J. Avery

19 So then, my beloved brethren, let every man be swift to hear, slow to speak, slow to wrath; 20 for the wrath of man does not produce the righteousness of God.
James 1:19-20

"Sometimes, your mind can be the hardest thing to keep open. Sometimes, your mouth can be the hardest thing to keep shut. All too often, these two problems coincide!" That is a personal quote that I wrote with this scripture in mind. How often do we live this scripture in reverse order? How often are we swift to speak, slow to hear, and easily angered?

Strengthening Your Walk with God is largely about maturity. It is about transitioning from learning about who and what God is—to actually internalizing and living out the precepts of His word. This scripture from God is capable of testing the most seasoned Christian, yet it needs to be followed. Listening is often the way we show respect and love; while avoiding anger is a sign of self-control and is frequently a manifestation of God's peace, in our hearts.

We live to please the Lord. We strive to work God's righteousness in our lives and the lives of others. Let us, beloved brethren, be a picture of mature Christianity. Let us be quick to listen, slow to speak, and hard ANGER.

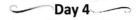 Day 4

Do Not Defile Yourself
By: Tamika & Mark J. Avery

15 There is nothing that enters a man from outside which can defile him; but the things which come out of him, those are the things that defile a man.
Mark 7:15

This teaching from Jesus, like many others, was a complete paradigm shift for God's people. It was a teaching unlike any other that they had ever heard from any religious teacher or prophet. What a man took into his body had always been subject to defile him, while speaking judgement and condemnation were common place and acceptable.

Even in the modern world, we struggle with the ramifications of this teaching. It is a man's heart that defiles him. It is a man's heart that brings forth *[...] evil thoughts, adulteries, fornications, murders, thefts, covetousness, wickedness, deceit, lewdness, an evil eye, blasphemy, pride, foolishness* (Mark 7:21-22). None of these are inherently found in any food we eat or liquid we drink. While watching what we eat and drink may make us healthier, it does not make us more righteous. That is a soul issue.

From a spiritual perspective, let us watch what comes out of our mouths, far more carefully than what we allow to enter them. Let us guard and care for our hearts far more than our bodies, as Jesus encourages us to do. Let us recognize and share what truly defiles a man, so that we can live Godlier lives and help others do the same. Speak truth. Speak life. Speak love. Amen? Amen!

⌐‿‿‿Day 5‿‿‿¬

Who Gave The Most?
By: Tamika & Mark J. Avery

1 And He looked up and saw the rich putting their gifts into the treasury, 2 and He saw also a certain poor widow putting in two mites. 3 So He said, "Truly I say to you that this poor widow has put in more than all; 4 for all these out of their abundance have put in offerings for God, but she out of her poverty put in all the livelihood that she had."
Luke 21:1-4

There are different views on money, religion, tithes and offering. They vary from denomination to denomination, church to church, and person to person. Many people struggle to understand the connection between God's Kingdom and worldly wealth.

The connection is a simple yet gets lost or overlooked. It is not the amount or frequency of money that pleases God, but the heart that gives. Why was Abel's offering better than Cain's (Genesis 4:2-7)? Why does the Lord love a cheerful giver (2 Corinthians 9:7)? Why did Jesus say a poor widow managed to give "more" than all of those rich men put together?

It is not about worldly value, size, or amount. God's measurement is about the heart. How much belief in God did it take for a poor old woman with no husband to give all she had? Knowing she would then have to trust God, completely, for her sustenance? She could have bought food. She could have attempted gamble, but instead she gave it to God and in doing so, she left herself completely at the mercy of His love. Jesus saw her heart, and He pointed it out as a lesson to those that chose to follow Him. Our giving is more about our hearts than the zeros in front of the decimals.

Giving
Thaddeus Miles
Photography

Day 6

God Does Not Keep Count!
By: Tamika & Mark J. Avery

21 Then Peter came to Him and said, "Lord, how often shall my brother sin against me, and I forgive him? Up to seven times?" 22 Jesus said to him, "I do not say to you, up to seven times, but up to seventy times seven.
Matthew 18:21-22

Alright, let's start with the math; seventy times seven will quickly give you four hundred and ninety, However, it is widely accepted that Jesus was not implying that we keep count and at the four hundredth and ninety first sin say, "I've got you now. I don't have to forgive you anymore!" It is much more likely that the point was that we should forgive as many times as we are sinned against.

Granted, the level Jesus points us too is extreme and will likely need to be grown into with God's help. Peter likely believed that he was being quite generous in asking if seven times was sufficient, until he heard Jesus' response. Today, let us focus on forgiving as many people as possible for as many sins against us as we can.

While presumably it will not number four hundred and ninety, it may try us just the same. It will help if we can keep in mind the amount of times God has forgiven us for our sins. Then remember that He has forgiven the sins, of not just us, but all of mankind. Surely, as we let our lights shine and give glory to our Creator, we can forgive those who shall trespass against us, in any given day. Amen?

Day 7

Repentance
By: Tamika & Mark J. Avery

6 All we like sheep have gone astray; We have turned, every one, to his own way; And the Lord has laid on Him the iniquity of us all.
Isaiah 53:6

Repentance is a process. It first requires that we admit that we are wrong and have made mistakes. Then we have to be deeply sorry or genuinely contrite. Lastly, must ask for forgiveness.

We have all gone astray; all sinned and come short of the glory of God. The consequences for our sins were placed on Jesus and He bore it for us all. It is because of us that Christ had to sacrifice himself. It is because of us that He had to endure those ordeals. Calvary was because of our iniquity, not His.

We are triumphant over death and sin; only because of God's love and Jesus' bloodshed. This is not because we are holy or righteous; not because we are so spiritually great that we saved ourselves. Today, as we count our blessings and thank God for life and favor, let us not forget repentance. There is only one that is good and it is not us. The God we serve should be the only thing that we take pride in. Let this be a day to be humble and repent before our Lord and Savior.

Day 8

That's A Stretch
By: Tamika & Mark J. Avery

1 I will bless the Lord at all times; His praise

shall continually be in my mouth.
Psalm 34:1

This verse seems like a bit of a hyperbole. Yes, it sounds good, but who can bless the Lord at "all" times and have His praise "continually" in their mouth? It seems like a stretch to say the least. Yet, when the rest of the psalm is read, the psalmist seems quite serious about the statement. It does not come across as exaggerated or insincere, in any way.

The more the psalm is read, the more the excitement and joy with which it was written comes through. The honesty and exuberance of the person who wrote this is admirable; it is attributed to King David. Maybe it is not just talk. Maybe it is a stretch, or maybe it will stretch us.

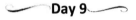 Day 9

That's A Stretch — Part 2
By: Tamika & Mark J. Avery

1 I will bless the Lord at all times; His praise
shall continually be in my mouth.
Psalm 34:1

Perhaps living out this verse is impossible, like perfection is beyond our grasp. However, what if like perfection, this scripture is worth pursuing, even if we fail. Knowing that we will never be perfect is no excuse for not trying as hard as possible to be better. We ask, "Can any harm come from setting this type of commitment to the Lord as our goal?" If we do fall short, will we not be closer to the goal for trying at all?

Certainly the one true God, our Lord and Savior is worthy of such devotion from us. At worst, we may be considered crazy for attempting the impossible, but we already know that all things are possible with God. Today, let us bless the Lord at all times. Let's keep His praise continually in our mouths. Should we fail, let us thank God for any improvement from the effort. Amen? Amen!

Day 10

True Worship
By: Tamika & Mark J. Avery

23 But the hour is coming, and now is, when the true worshipers will worship the Father in spirit and truth; for the Father is seeking such to worship Him. 24 God is Spirit, and those who worship Him must worship in spirit and truth.
John 4:23-24

Worship is most often defined as a show of reverence and/or adoration. It makes perfect sense that we would worship God. He gave us life and sustains us. It is His kingdom that we are hopeful to enter when our life here ends. Reverence and adoration are surely in order, but how do we worship properly?

Take the rest of your devotional time today and write your definition of worship. We will revisit this tomorrow.

_____
_____
_____
_____
_____
_____
_____
_____
_____
_____

Day 11

True Worship — Part 2
By: Tamika & Mark J. Avery

23 But the hour is coming, and now is, when the true
worshipers will worship the Father in spirit and truth;
for the Father is seeking such to worship Him. 24 God
is Spirit, and those who worship Him must worship
in spirit and truth.
John 4:23-24

The scripture implies that there are true and false ways to
worship. How do we know the difference? How do we get this
right? God is a Spirit and "true" worship is in spirit and in truth,
but what does that mean?

The answer may lie in another set of scriptures. Mark 7:6-7
reads, *He answered and said to them, well did Isaiah prophesy
of you hypocrites, as it is written: 'This people honors Me with
their lips, but their heart is far from Me. And in vain they
worship Me, Teaching as doctrines the commandments of men.'*
So, obviously worship can be done in vain, but this may also be
the key to doing it right.

Would you like to revise your definition of worship from
yesterday? If necessary, think on it throughout the day and we
will finish this tomorrow.

_____

_____

_____

_____

_____

Day 12

True Worship, Part 3
By: Tamika & Mark J. Avery

23 But the hour is coming, and now is, when the true worshipers will worship the Father in spirit and truth; for the Father is seeking such to worship Him. 24 God is Spirit, and those who worship Him must worship in spirit and truth.
John 4:23-24

What if worshipping in spirit is just that, spiritual? Is love (Agape) spiritual or physical? Is prayer spiritual or physical? What if true worship comes from that spiritual place that love and prayer spring from? What if worshipping in truth is about connecting our hearts to God, more than just lifting up our voices or opening our wallets? What if praising Him with our lips or giving our money without our hearts being near Him is what the people in the book of Mark were guilty of that invalidated their worship?

Are we singing because we are at that part of the church service or because the joy of the Lord is bursting from our hearts? Are we tithing because we are told too, but not as a true love offering for the Lord? Has our worship become and in some cases always been about the traditions around us, rather than a genuine outpouring of love and appreciation to the Lord? Let us examine whether or not we are true worshippers today or if we are missing the mark. God deserves true worship in spirit and in truth. <u>Let us give it to Him</u> and apply what you have learned over the last three days in your worship time.

Day 13

Cleansed!
By: Adrienne Goodlow

9 Do you not know that the unrighteous will not inherit the kingdom of God? Do not be deceived. Neither fornicators, nor idolaters, nor adulterers, nor homosexuals, nor sodomites, 10 nor thieves, nor covetous, nor drunkards, nor revilers, nor ex-tortioners will inherit the kingdom of God. 11 And such were some of you. But you were washed, … . sanctified, … justified in the name of the Lord Jesus and by the Spirit of our God.
1 Corinthians 6:9-11

Most folk believe these scriptures are meant as a correction for someone who does not know Christ or whose life reflects that they have not accepted Him fully. However, they were a reminder for me! These scriptures are speaking to the things we once were but are no longer, because of our relationship with Christ. These words are there to help us to appreciate the provision that was made for us to be "right" in the eyes of our loving Father who gave His only begotten son so that we may have life. By the spirit of a GOD who loves us unconditionally, we have been taken from a place of sin and have been made clean. I entitled this as "Cleansed" which is past tense. That means once we accepted Jesus as our Lord and Savior, the work of being made holy was accomplished in us once and for all.

From what do you need God to cleanse you?

_____
_____
_____
_____
_____

Day 14

Cleansed! — Part 2

By: Adrienne Goodlow

9 Do you not know that the unrighteous will not inherit the kingdom of God? Do not be deceived. Neither fornicators, nor idolaters, nor adulterers, nor homosexuals, nor sodomites, 10 nor thieves, nor covetous, nor drunkards, nor revilers, nor extortioners will inherit the kingdom of God. 11 And such were some of you. But you were washed, but you were sanctified, but you were justified in the name of the Lord Jesus and by the Spirit of our God.

1 Corinthians 6:9-11

Not once did we read that Jesus had to go back and redo any miracle He performed in Bible. He is good and perfect in every way and therefore once He died for each and every one of us, we were truly saved. However, there is a call to action here, there is something that we ourselves must do to be in "right" standing with GOD. The list of things that would keep us from inheriting the kingdom of GOD was present tense; however, the scriptures go on to state, *and such WERE some of you*. This means we have to put those behaviors behind us. Those thoughts, that speech, those actions that would qualify you as a fornicator, idolater, adulterer etc., would have to be in the past. Friends, I encourage you today to call on the holy name of Jesus and receive Him in your heart and work diligently to slay the old man within you that would keep you from the kingdom of GOD. Know that He died for YOU, once and for all. Use the word to exhort and encourage one another, know that there is a hope and a promise for each and every one of us!

— Day 15 —

GOD, The Abundant Giver
By: Adrienne Goodlow

10 Now may He who supplies seed to the sower, and bread for food, supply and multiply the seed you have sown and increase the fruits of your righteousness, 11 while you are enriched in everything for all liberality, which causes thanksgiving through us to God.
2 Corinthians 9:10-11

GOD our Father is the ultimate giver. In the above scriptures, He is inciting each of us to give, so that He can give us yet even more than we can imagine. When reading the surrounding scriptures (2 Corinthians 9:6-15) this giving is a cheerful giving and it states that we will reap accordingly (basically, we will receive according to our giving). GOD wants us to give generously so He can bless us generously. He does not command that we give "generously," for it states *each man should give what He decided in his heart to give.* However, He tells us in His word that *you will be made rich in every way so that you can be generous on every occasion.*

This takes the guess work out of what it takes to please our Father. In 2 Corinthians 9:13 it lets us know that due to our service (generosity), *men will praise GOD.* Is that not what our main purpose in life is about? It is about pleasing GOD and showing others the way to Him and in our giving, GOD will be praised. Although giving is only one facet of our service to GOD, it yields great rewards from our beautiful Father, as it prompts Him to give to us *surpassing grace*; surpassing to me means above and beyond what is expected. So be encouraged, GOD sees all you do (tithes, offerings, volunteering, helping your neighbor, sharing, etc.) and will bless you often times more abundantly than what you can imagine, because it is from grace that He lovingly and abundantly gives.

⌒⌒⌒Day 16⌒⌒⌒

A Love So Deep
By: Adrienne Goodlow

7 But the very hairs of your head are all numbered. Do not fear therefore; you are of more value than many sparrows.
Luke 12:7

My friends, who of us can say we love someone so deeply that we will count the number of hairs on their head? Be mindful, that we would have to count multiple times a day; as human hairs shed throughout the day and we often may not have the same number at the end of the day as the amount we started with. That would also mean that we would have to be with them every second of the day to know exactly when the numbers of hairs changed. For you to count the hair of someone is a deep love and would also mean that you will also keep up with their feelings, their health, and their thoughts, etc.

This is how GOD loves us. He is with us every millisecond of our lives and cares so much for us that even the things about us that are expendable, like our hair, He knows about it. This is so amazing to me because these are the words of Jesus, GOD's only begotten son, who died for us, so there is no room for doubt.

Love.

Day 17

A Love So Deep — Part 2
By: Adrienne Goodlow

7 But the very hairs of your head are all numbered. Do not fear therefore; you are of more value than many sparrows.
Luke 12:7

We are often moved to tears and thankful when we see an expression of love in a movie or when a loved one expresses their love for us. How much more so should we be filled with an overwhelming gratitude and joy, when we truly understand how deep GOD's love is for us. This knowing the number of hairs on our head is just the surface of His love, there is not room enough in this devotional to speak on the sacrifices, the patience and the grace that GOD has shown to express His love for each and every one of us.

I encourage you to take a moment today and just focus on being loved down to the number of hairs on your body. Feel it and embrace it to the best of your ability. Now think on how you can show GOD how you love Him and then let His spirit guide you in paying it forward. Be blessed and encouraged.

_____
_____
_____
_____
_____
_____
_____
_____
_____
_____

⌒〜Day 18〜⌒

Anointed and Appointed
By: Adrienne Goodlow

27 But the anointing which you have received from Him abides in you, and you do not need that anyone teach you; but as the same anointing teaches you concerning all things, and is true, and is not a lie, and just as it has taught you, you will abide in Him.
1 John 2:27

My friends, you have been anointed, and as this scripture points out, it was a real anointing. There is a great work in you that GOD has placed and anointed so that you can accomplish the GOD glorifying dream He put in you. The scripture also states that you do not need anyone to teach you, trust and believe, you have a direct line to our Father. You do not need someone to speak over you to tell you that you are anointed, for your Heavenly Father as already told you so. You have everything you need in you to start that ministry, business or whatever He placed on your heart to do to help others.

Get in that quiet place, commune with our Father, let Him speak directly to you then go forth and do that great work you were created to do.

⌒〜Day 19〜⌒

Surrounded by The Mountain
By: Adrienne Goodlow

1 A Song of Ascents. Those who trust in the Lord Are like Mount Zion, Which cannot be moved, but abides forever. 2 As

the mountains surround Jerusalem, So the Lord surrounds His
people From this time forth and forever.

Psalm 125: 1-2

Who of us can physically move a mountain? For many of us, a
boulder can be a challenge, so to move a mountain would take
supernatural power. So like the mountain that cannot be
moved, when you trust in the Lord and He surrounds you like
an unmovable mountain, you are truly protected forever and
ever.

With all the things that we face today, financial issues, health
challenges and lack of moral standards in this world, we need
supernatural protection more than ever. Spiritual warfare has
been declared on GOD's people and He vows to surround and
protect those that trust Him like a mountain!

Just imagine an immovable and constantly changing mountain
protecting you from someone who is trying to harm you. No
matter what they try, the mountain would change to thwart
their efforts; a snow storm or an avalanche, whatever it takes
to keep your enemy at bay. That is the mountain we find in the
LORD, no matter the challenges the adversary tries to throw our
way, we can be assured that the Mountain of the LORD that
surrounds us will always and forever more protect us, when we
trust in him.

⌐───Day 20 ───⌐

First Steps
By: Adrienne Goodlow

23 The steps of a good man are ordered by the Lord, And He
delights in his way. 24 Though he fall, he shall not be utterly
cast down; For the Lord upholds him with His hand.

Psalm 37: 23-24

There is nothing more exciting for a parent, than to watch their child take their first steps; whether it's their first child or their fifth. They rejoice in seeing the baby begin to walk, not only to do something they have never done before, but walking will forever and inevitably change the baby's life. So our Heavenly Father rejoices when we take our first steps toward Him. When we begin to walk in the way in which the Father has ordered, it's like seeing His baby walk for the first time and He rejoices as He knows our lives will be changed forever, for the good.

What things should you walk away from and what things should you walk toward?

_____

_____

_____

_____

_____

— Day 21

First Steps — Part 2
By: Adrienne Goodlow

23 The steps of a good man are ordered by the Lord, And He delights in his way. 24 Though he fall, he shall not be utterly cast down; For the Lord upholds him with His hand.
Psalm 37: 23-24

When a baby first learns to walk, there are stumbles and tumbles until the process is mastered and then the child takes off running. This is paralleled to our walk in serving GOD. We may stumble and tumble and as the scriptures state, *though we may fall,* we are not counted out or *cast down.* We get back up and continue to work to master the process.

Like a loving parent with outstretched hands, to catch a wobbling child, so does the Lord hold out His hand to catch us when we stumble or fall. At these times He upholds us, so that we are encouraged to continue on our spiritual journey.

Day 22

The Midas Touch
By: Adrienne Goodlow

10 The thief does not come except to steal, and to kill, and to destroy. I have come that they may have life, and that they may have it more abundantly.
John 10:10

Anything you do, anything you touch, or anything you involve yourself with, you should do it with the motivation to improve it. Thus you will create a better product or provide a great service, that will become a great benefit for those it affects.

I was content with just writing this devotional, until I was also blessed with the honor of talking to a dear spiritual friend with whom I shared it. As we spoke further and she confirmed some things spiritually, another golden nugget was provided and this particular scripture came to mind.

Meditate on it:

_____
_____
_____
_____
_____
_____
_____

⸺Day 23⸺

The Midas Touch — Part 2
By: Adrienne Goodlow

10 The thief does not come except to steal, and to kill, and to destroy. I have come that they may have life, and that they may have it more abundantly.
John 10:10

After meditation the connection came to me. Jesus came to improve our lives; this is the epitome of the Midas Touch. He came so that we can have a better life. Everything He touched was left with a residue of great value, much greater than gold which is deemed a precious commodity. When we put this in effect in our lives, we are indeed living out the life GOD so lovingly designed for us; that is to walk and talk in the image of Jesus. Just the very opposite of what the adversary came to do.

We all know the story ended sadly, as the king's touch turned his child to a golden statue; as his intent was to gain riches only for himself. However, if you humbly work to improve circumstances for people, and give the glory to the ultimate provider of all things, your story will have a kingdom ending.

As I strive to work and live by this precious golden Word GOD has given me, I just wanted to share it with you as I value you and what I am learning. Cherish this Word.

⸺Day 24⸺

Thankful For Prayer
By: Adrienne Goodlow

6 Be anxious for nothing, but in everything by prayer and supplication, with thanksgiving, let your requests

be made known to God;
Philippians 4:6

In this season of THANKSGIVING, DON'T WORRY. Worry is fear and fear is NOT of GOD. Pray about all things. When concerns come up, say a prayer. Take a deep breath and say a quick word to cast away worry, as it is only a peace thief. GOD has made it so that we can be in relationship with Him. He wants to be more than just a Genie in a bottle; He wants to be your best friend, confidant, everything because you are already His everything! There is no love greater than His and who better to help you and guide you with your concerns than the creator.

When approaching Him in prayer:
- Thank Him for His answer and His help through it all.
- Thank Him for the wisdom to pursue Him in all things.
- Thank Him for what He has already done and the promises of what He will do.
- Thank Him for taking away the worry and replacing it with "the peace" that surpasses ALL understanding.

I promise you, by the time you finish thanking him, you won't have a worry to speak on because you have already thanked Him for His solutions. Although He invites us to approach Him with supplication, make your prayers, prayers of faith and declaration. <u>Faith pleases him, and that is our top priority</u>.

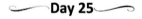 **Day 25**

Complete In Christ
By: Adrienne Goodlow

9 For in Him dwells all the fullness of the Godhead bodily; 10 and you are complete in Him, who is the head of all principality and power.
Colossians 2:9-10

When something is complete, it lacks nothing or "no thing." To be complete in Christ, means that you are not lacking in anything. You are covered in grace and mercy and seen complete through Jesus in the eyes of our loving Father. The very reason Jesus came to earth was to atone for our sins so that we will be whole, lacking nothing! Be steadfast in your belief in the Savior. Allow Him to be the Lord of your life. If you can truly conceive what it means to be complete in Christ, you will be able to speak to the issues of your life in confidence; knowing that the power of Christ over ALL things is within you, making you complete, and you will lack "no thing."

Day 26

Be Comforted
By: Tamika & Mark J. Avery

38 For I am persuaded that neither death nor life, nor angels nor principalities nor powers, nor things present nor things to come, 39 nor height nor depth, nor any other created thing, shall be able to separate us from the love of God which is in Christ Jesus our Lord.
Romans 8:38-39

This is such a comforting set of scriptures. Paul probably meant it to be just that. Most Christians, at some point, come to the realization that giving their life to God does not keep bad things from happening. Depending on who you believe, it may actually bring more problems into your life.

It is quite a list Paul lays out at the beginning of the verse: death, life, angels, principalities, powers, things present, things future, highs, lows, and any other creature. All of these things will affect us in different ways. All may come against us and make it more difficult to follow God and trust Him at times.

The comfort is in the fact that, try as they may, none of these things is actually capable of separating us from the love of God. Death cannot do it. Angels cannot do it. Principalities and powers cannot do it. Highs and lows cannot do it. Think of "love of God" as a place that we are in and though some things may affect us, they cannot remove us from this spot. We just have to endure and if we do not faint, we will receive our reward. How comforting is that?

 Day 27

The Source
By: Tamika & Mark J. Avery

38 He who believes in Me, as the Scripture has said, out of his heart will flow rivers of living water.
John 7:38

Christianity is about giving. It begins with what God gives us (life, grace, mercy, love, etc.). We in turn give back to God (praise, worship, reverence, love, etc.). We also give to each other (service, time, love, etc.). God is God; so His supplies are endless, but in giving, how do "we" avoid running out?

If we simply give from our own stockpiles, no matter how well supplied we are, we will eventually run out. Wells run dry. Cupboards become empty. Spiritually it is no different. We are simply finite creatures; it is in our nature.

The answer to our supply problem is that we connect to God, who never runs out of anything. So why do we sometimes still feel disconnected? Sin is the problem. Sin has disconnected us from the Lord. The answer? Belief in Jesus. We bridge the gap that sin created and connect to God through Jesus.

Day 28

The Source — Part 2
By: Tamika & Mark J. Avery

38 He who believes in Me, as the Scripture has said, out of his heart will flow rivers of living water.
John 7:38

With our connection to God, we now have living water flowing from deep within us. It springs from a spiritual place within our spirits, allowing us to quench the thirst of all that seek life. It will never run dry or stop flowing as long as we stay connected to its source (God). God gives to us that we may give to others. Let us connect to the source today and quench the thirst, from the Lord's spring.

Take a moment and just talk to God.

_____
_____
_____
_____
_____

Day 29

A Penny's Worth
By: Tamika & Mark J. Avery

1 For the kingdom of heaven is like a landowner who went out early in the morning to hire laborers for his vineyard. 2 Now when he had agreed with the laborers for a denarius a day, he sent them into his vineyard.
Matthew 20:1-2

Heaven is God's kingdom. There is a mansion there with many rooms and God can invite whomever He sees fit to live there. We are beyond blessed to be offered the opportunity to spend eternity with God and still, sometimes we grumble.

In this parable the householder is God, the labourers are us, and the penny is Heaven. God has agreed to give Heaven to us if we work for Him and we accepted. Note that no one in the parable complained about their pay (up front) or the work to be done.

There was no problem until it came time their agreed upon compensation. Every man received exactly what was agreed upon, but some of them were not happy. The ones that had worked the longest felt cheated or slighted in some way. They felt that perhaps the householder should have increased their pay or lowered the workers' pay that joined later in the day.

We must avoid the danger of comparison and judgment. We are all in the same boat. We are all working for God for our heavenly reward. None of us are any worthier than the next man or woman, no matter how long or hard we feel that we have been working. None of us should look down on anyone else for any reason. If anything, we should be lifting our fellow laborers up, for the harvest is plentiful, but the laborers are few. Let us seek to strengthen each other, as we seek to strengthen ourselves. There are enough pennies for everyone. Let us labor in harmony, rather than discord.

— Day 30 —

The End
By: Tamika & Mark J. Avery

7 I have fought the good fight, I have finished the race, I have kept the faith. 8 Finally, there is laid up for me the crown of

righteousness, which the Lord, the righteous Judge, will give to me on that Day, and not to me only but also to all who have loved His appearing.

2 Timothy 4:7-8

As we close the month of November, we want to touch on the end of our walks, as Christians. Everything that has a beginning has an ending and life is no exception. Paul wrote these words to Timothy, presumably realizing that he was close to the end of his life.

Honestly, we believe that this should be the hope and goal for every Christian. To be able to say, if given the opportunity, that we have fought a good fight and finished our course having kept the faith.   Therefore, the Lord awaits us with crowns of righteousness, because we have loved Him and served Him that well.

There is no fear of death in these words. There is no sign of defeat or disappointment, over failed assignments or uncompleted tasks. There is no doubt in his words about God's pleasure with Him and his efforts for Him.   We are strengthening our walk with God in the hopes of arriving at the place that Paul finds himself in these scriptures; prepared to meet his maker and give an account of his life.

We pray that: *May we all be so blessed, when our time of departure is at hand. May God bless and keep us all, as we strive to bless and keep others, in Jesus' name, Amen.*

December

By: Ayani_Meli

Day 1

Clean your House

12 For we do not wrestle against flesh and blood, but against principalities, against powers, against the rulers of the darkness of this age, against spiritual hosts of wickedness in the heavenly places.
Ephesians 6:12

This country is being torn apart by hatred, greed, anger and sin. How do we fix it? Each person must start with their own Heart; i.e., the spiritual house. Guarding your heart, allows you greater focus (mental house). When your mind is settled, you have more control over your temple (flesh house). When your flesh is under subjection, it is easier to get a handle on your household (physical house). Guarding your heart is the key to all of your houses.

Watch the things you allow yourself to do to the temple. In short, guard your ear gates, eye gates and mouth. Do not allow negative speech to lead you into a place not destined and ordered by God. If every individual used all their keys, the world would be a better place. Start today; it's not too late, the first day, of the last month of the year. Lock things down. Clean up the clutter and toss out the trash! Clean your house.

Day 2

Be Aware

10 Finally, my brethren, be strong in the Lord and in the power of His might. 11 Put on the whole armor of God, that you may be able to stand against the wiles of the devil.
Ephesians 6:10-11

As a believer who has embraced salvation, you cannot be possessed, but can be oppressed and influenced by spirits in your presence. That is why it is important to keep your mind stayed on God. He who dwells within you is greater than He who dwells without. Don't allow petty people or situations that have been skewed against you, to take you out of your character. The enemy is out to destroy you and your household. Put on your armor every day. There is too much at stake to go without protection.

 Day 3

A smile is Worth a Thousand Words

31 Let all bitterness, wrath, anger, clamor, and evil speaking be put away from you, with all malice. 32 And be kind to one another, tenderhearted, forgiving one another, just as God in Christ forgave you.
Ephesians 4:31-32

Are you sorry when you push someone else's buttons? Try putting yourself in their shoes. How would you feel? Pain is not easy to bear, especially when unwarranted. Depending on your life experiences, kindness must be practiced. Make it a habit. It takes about two weeks of consistent behavior for something to become a habit. Remember, it costs us nothing to smile. That one smile might just turn someone else's day around.

A BEAUTIFUL SMILE IS WORTH
A THOUSAND WORDS

Day 4

The Power of the Tongue

> 18 There is one who speaks like the piercings of a sword, But the tongue of the wise promotes health.
> Proverbs 12:18

In retrospect, I can see that a parent's words were a powerful blessing or a curse against our lives and accomplishments. Some had supportive authority figures growing up and some did not. Can you look back and see some of the mistakes they made? Endeavor not to do the same thing. We must remember to speak life over not only ourselves, our children and our households but over other people and situations. Think about the words that came out of your mouth yesterday. Were they positive and uplifting? Did they tear someone down or hurt their feelings? Did you speak negatively about your family, children or finances? This must stop.

Whatever you build up, you will ultimately reap from it. Every blessing in your life was placed there for a reason. Don't curse them. Speak death; reap death. SPEAK LIFE; REAP LIFE.

Day 5

Pray Much?

> The Lord is near to all who call upon Him, To all who call upon Him in truth.
> Psalm 145:18

When we pray, we commune with God. Quite often, things and opportunities come to cause us to invoke or want to activate our prayer life. My dad used to say, "much prayer, much power." That is entirely the truth. Prayer opens up that spiritual conduit between us and Abba. It also shifts the atmosphere, having a direct impact on the activity of the angels assigned to us and the demons sent to destroy us. That thought alone should drive you to your prayer closet at every opportunity.

However, this is the thought for today. If we dig deeper, a much more substantial statement is, "much prayer, deeper intimacy." As humans, we crave intimacy. It is essential to our mental and SPIRITUAL well-being. There is no greater love than the Love of God. Succinctly, there is no greater intimacy, than intimacy with God. Love covers a multitude of sins. Prayer activates, deepens and strengthens that love.

Prayer results in direction, clarification and intimacy. Can you ask for anything more?

— Day 6 —

Like Jesus

6 He who says he abides in Him ought himself also to
walk just as He walked.
1 John 2:6

If someone walked up to you and espoused the popular slogan of a sneaker company, you would know immediately what they were talking about. You would know that it would take hard work, it may not be glamorous, but you would strive to do it anyway. So if I walked up to you and said just do it, just be like Jesus, what would your immediate reaction be? Would you know how to go about it? Would you desire to accomplish it? The Bible tells us in various passages of Scripture, to be like Him; to be made in His image. What must you change to take a step in that direction? Do it. Walk like him. Talk like him. Be like him.

List some ways that you can be like Jesus today.

_____

_____

_____

_____

_____

_____

_____

_____

_____

_____

_____

_____

Day 7

Internal Balance

**2 Beloved, I pray that you may prosper in all things and be in health, just as your soul prospers.
3 John 1:2**

Don't allow outside influences to upset the balance in your life. Your internal balance and peace of mind are important to your survival; i.e., spiritually, mentally and physically. Distractions will manifest. Sometimes they will come hard and fast. Other times they may sneak up on you at a snail's pace. The enemy is true to his character and will sometimes use those people and situations close to your heart. Whatever the enemy brings to you, is designed to cause you to forget who you are, forget who God is, and lose your peace.

Day 8

Positive Vibes

7 Do not be deceived, God is not mocked; for whatever a man sows, that he will also reap. 8 For he who sows to his flesh will of the flesh reap corruption, but he who sows to the Spirit will of the Spirit reap everlasting life.
Galatians 6:7

The Word also says, *out of an abundance of the heart, the mouth speaks.* If filth and hatred come out of your mouth, filth and hatred will dominate your life. When you exude positive vibes, you do not have to be surprised at what comes back to you. Sometimes we mope around and complain about the way we are being treated. Take stock, how are you treating the people you feel are doing you wrong? You are the only person you can control. However, if everyone lived by that tenet, the world would be a much more beautiful place. The enemy does not control everything in this universe. God is the Supreme Being. There are people who still believe in God. There are people who still trust in God. Don't just say it, live like one of those people.

Day 9

Auditions or Tests

7 Jesus said to him, "It is written again, 'You shall not tempt the Lord your God.' " 8 Again, the devil took Him up on an exceedingly high mountain, and showed Him all the kingdoms of the world and their glory. 9 And he said to Him, "All these things I will give You if You will fall down and worship me." 10 Then Jesus said to him, "Away with you, Satan! For it is written,

> 'You shall worship the Lord your God, and Him
> only you shall serve.'"
> **Matthew 4:7-10**

Auditions are simply tests. In the natural, those tests are designed to ascertain your skills, state of mind and potential for development. There are good auditions and bad. How many times have you been auditioned and did not know it? You just knew that you were in an uncomfortable situation. We don't like it when it's done to us, but we like to do it to God. It wasn't fair to you and it's not fair to God. Do not make God audition for you!

Satan wanted to make God jump through hoops by tempting Jesus. His end game was to force God to save Jesus. But Jesus spat the Word in satan's face and remained true to who He was made manifest in the flesh to be, the Son of God. Jesus had <u>no doubt</u> about His dignity, His character or His purpose. He Himself, had no reason to test God. Neither do you in a negative way.

⌁ **Day 10** ⌁

Auditions or Tests — Part 2

> 7 Jesus said to him, "It is written again, 'You shall not tempt the Lord your God.' " 8 Again, the devil took Him up on an exceedingly high mountain, and showed Him all the kingdoms of the world and their glory. 9 And he said to Him, "All these things I will give You if You will fall down and worship me." 10 Then Jesus said to him, "Away with you, Satan! For it is written, 'You shall worship the Lord your God, and Him only you shall serve.'"
> **Matthew 4:7-10**

It is ok to test God according to His Word; because He will prevail. But when that test is rooted in doubt, then you have a serious issue. He has nothing to prove to us. We cast shadows of our humanity onto God, in the way that we handle our relationship with him. Don't give God ultimatums (tests) and attempt to relate to Him like you would a human. God knows you; He designed you. Peter denied Him, but he still was able to fulfill his kingdom destiny. He knows your darkest thoughts, wants and desires; and loves us in spite of them. Because things do not always work the way that you want them to, is no reason to act like a bad child and test God. If it is not in His Will, it is not going to happen. He may have something better in store.

—— Day 11 ——

Allow Those Seeds To Be Watered

5 Who then is Paul, and who is Apollos, but ministers through whom you believed, as the Lord gave to each one? 6 I plant-ed, Apollos watered, but God gave the increase. 7 So then neither he who plants is anything, nor he who waters, but God who gives the increase.
1 Corinthians 3:5-7

Dr. Mike Murdock says "you cannot learn from anyone you resent." Extrapolating on that and taking it a step further, resentment is like a cancer. You cannot wholly love anyone you resent. Take that resentment and throw it in the enemies' face. It is only exists to keep you from receiving wisdom from the people God put in your life, to water seeds you received long ago. Seeds can and will rot. The Word of God will not be destroyed, but it can rot from your heart and your spirit. When the Word comes to you, don't resent the messenger and reject the Word. You will be rejecting the living water and allowing the seeds to rot.

Day 12

Contentment

2 He makes me to lie down in green pastures; He leads me beside the still waters.
Psalms 23 2

During a broadcast, Bishop J Richard Evans advised us to exchange God's peace for our pressure. Everything we need rests in God. He has it all and can provide it all. He is just waiting for us to ask; seek it out. We have not, because we ask not. Our lives are filled with clutter which affects our consciousness. Sometimes we can't sleep, because we cannot shut our "mind" off. When your space is cluttered; your mind is cluttered. Declutter your life, and subsequently declutter your mind. It works. I just tried it. The feeling of freedom was phenomenal. I am now more productive, focused and able to "hear" God just a little bit clearer.

Contentment: Day 735
Thaddeus Miles Photography

Day 13

Labels

Do not allow others to label you. In searching for scriptures about who God says we are, I found the following:

I am a child of God.
John 1:12
I am a branch of the true vine, and a conduit of Christ's life.
John 15:1-5

I am a friend of Jesus.
John 15:15

I have been justified and redeemed.
Romans 3:23-24; Romans 6:6

I will not be condemned by God, I have been set free from the law of sin and death.
Romans 8:1-2

As a child of God, I am a fellow heir with Christ.
Romans 8:17

Make these affirmations today! And add your own.

I don't need you to label me, I can do just fine by myself: Faithful. Honest. Truthful. Loving. Kind. Author. Mother. Believer. Publisher.

Who are you?

_____
_____
_____
_____
_____
_____
_____

Day 14

The Peace of God

7 And the peace of God, which transcends all understanding, will guard your hearts and your minds in Christ Jesus.
Philippians 4:7

Do you know what THE PEACE OF GOD really feels like? Have you ever been close to experiencing it? The best definition is this: going through an emotionally, physically or financially harrowing experience and trusting that His Will is being done. When you can step back and say "Lord let your Will be done" and absolutely mean it, that is the peace of God.

Think about that definition for the rest of the day and stop worrying about things you cannot change. Ask for His peace.

Where do you need His peace?

_____

_____

_____

_____

_____

Day 15

The Peace of God — Part 2

7 And the peace of God, which transcends all understanding, will guard your hearts and your minds in Christ Jesus.
Philippians 4:7

Did you ask for His peace? Has it begun to manifest yet? Have you yielded your troubles to Him yet?

Let me share my biggest test (trouble) with you. My dad was my best friend; my ride or die. We went to church, shopping and just about any other place that he needed help. He had some physical challenges and I always wanted to be there to pick up the slack. When he went to preach, I was there. The only place I could not go was when he was doing something related to the church, in terms of carpentry. December 2004, my best friend all but transitioned into heaven in my arms. I was broken. But I was not destroyed and I realized that with his transition came the Peace of God. I was not destroyed and the spirit of grief did not rest perpetually on my life. I missed him terribly, but I also saw God begin to repair the broken relationship with my mother. All of the animosity and ill feelings the enemy wanted me to have toward her, vanished. I had moments of grief, but I knew, beyond a shadow of a doubt, that everything was going to be alright. I accepted His peace and learned to trust HIM.

Peace Looks Good on You
Thaddeus Miles Photography

Don't Stumble

16 for though a righteous man falls seven times, he rises
again, but the wicked are brought down by calamity.
17 Do not gloat when your enemy falls; when he
stumbles, do not let your heart rejoice,
Proverbs 24:16-17

Society has subtly taught us to be selfish or self-oriented. Most of us will flatly deny that, but often we definitely want what we want. This behavior did not start when we were adults, it started when we were children. If we are not aware of this fact, we are doomed to stumble on our walk. This same ideology causes us to color outside of the lines. As a young adult, a child of about four taught me a lesson. She asked me nicely for snack. I proceeded to give her six cookies. She would not take them. I asked why? She said, "my mommy only allows me to have three." I said, "well this time it won't matter." She declined. Surely enough, that was the recommended serving.

Those cookies were like the Word. We teach our children to go after what they want. But sometimes we don't give them enough guidelines. How often do we read the bible to them? They hear it on Sunday morning or during children's church, but never at home. That behavior compounds as we get older. So, we begin to interpret God's instructions for daily living the way we desire to interpret them. Embracing the part we like and changing or revising the part that we don't like. The Word won't teach us to be selfish OR SELF ORIENTED in any regard. Don't stumble. God is the only one who can keep us all from stumbling.

Day 17

Your Dusty Life

3 And why do you look at the speck in your brother's eye, but do not consider the plank in your own eye? 4 Or how can you say to your brother, 'Let me remove the speck from your eye'; and look, a plank is in your own eye? 5 Hypocrite! First remove the plank from your own eye, and then you will see clearly to remove the speck from your brother's eye.

Matthew 7:3-5

Good things that happen in your life, were designed just for you. People on the outside looking in, think that you have it all together. They cannot see the cracks in your foundation. The things with which you struggle. You look good every Sunday. But there is a fine layer of dust (sin) covering your person; invisible to the physical eye but not the spiritual eye. Be aware that because you have favor, is no reason to look down on other people. Everyone's life experience is different. Sometimes others make decisions that don't meet your standards. How do you react? How does God react when we sin? Do you hold it against them? Forgetting that you made that same mistake a few years prior? Before you judge others, take a good long look in the mirror and ask yourself, NO, ask God what you need to do to look more like Him.

Day 18

Your Dusty Life — Part 2

3 And why do you look at the speck in your brother's eye, but do not consider the plank in your own eye? 4 Or how can you say to your brother, 'Let me remove the speck from your eye'; and look, a plank is in your own eye? 5 Hypocrite! First remove

the plank from your own eye, and then you will see clearly to remove the speck from your brother's eye.
Matthew 7:3-5

What hidden sin lurks in your life? What dust covers you and has clouded your vision? After you pray, ask God what you need to change or work on and list it below. Be sure to revisit this from time to time, so that you can see your progress toward looking more like Him.

_____

_____

_____

_____

_____

_____

_____

_____

—— Day 19 ——

Love Conquers All

44 But I say to you, love your enemies, bless those who curse you, do good to those who hate you, and pray for those who spitefully use you and persecute you,
Matthew 5:44

Looking back over some lines of prose that were written a while ago. These words popped out at me: *There is always a smile somewhere in my spirit, it just gets lost sometimes.* It was referring to the strained relationships that I've had with some family members.

How do you love somebody that hates you? Some would argue that it is easier to love a stranger than those who are closest to us but treat us like an enemy. A few years ago a school counselor told me that those in our inner circle can hurt us more than strangers. That has proven itself correct time and again. If you look closely at the scripture, it covers everyone; enemies, frenemies, strangers and family. If you are going through this, it should keep you in prayer, not walking in bitterness and unforgiveness. Change your attitude and the antics they pull will not bother you. Decide to love them anyway and watch your world get just a little bit brighter. Love conquers all. Maybe not today or tomorrow, but you will have more peace of mind.

— Day 20 —

Who Is Your Master

10 For do I now persuade men, or God? Or do I seek to please men? For if I still pleased men, I would not be a bondservant of Christ.
Galatians 1:10

This scripture oddly brings to mind the old adage "you cannot serve two masters." Is man or God the head of your life? Man does not have dominion over heaven, only earth. You must live your life serving, glorifying, magnifying and adoring the One who has dominion over heaven. Emotionally abusive relationships are not healthy. Man is fickle and will find a reason to put conditions on his love. You cannot live up to your full potential in the kingdom trying to please man. You don't need man's approval or verification. The only thing you need is God. He desires a deeply spiritual and intimate relationship with you. God loves unconditionally. Become totally immersed in God and allow Him to overwhelm you with His love.

Day 21

Secret Sins

15 who show the work of the law written in their hearts, their conscience also bearing witness, and between themselves their thoughts accusing or else excusing them) 16 in the day when God will judge the secrets of men by Jesus Christ, according to my gospel.
Romans 2:15-16

Scandalous obsession pervades our society; from popular television shows, to book covers, to wanton displays of affection. Folk just cannot seem to get enough of watching, hearing about or writing about lust, greed, hatred, malicious acts and so forth. What scandalous obsession are you hiding? Can you give up your scandalous obsession, you know that thing that you know is wrong but you keep doing anyway? Let's take it down a notch. Maybe you don't have an obsession, but just some scandalous behavior. Are you prone to the occasional "little white lie?" Well, a lie is a lie. Lies don't have colors. A lie is sin. SIN DOESN'T HAVE COLORS. Lust is sin. Greed is sin. Murder is sin. You get the point. Secret sin destroys lives and it destroys souls.

Do you have secret sins that you struggle with? How can you change this?

_____
_____
_____
_____
_____
_____
_____
_____

Day 22

Secret Sins — Part 2

15 who show the work of the law written in their hearts, their conscience also bearing witness, and between themselves their thoughts accusing or else excusing them) 16 in the day when God will judge the secrets of men by Jesus Christ, according to my gospel.

Romans 2:15-16

We like to categorize sin, as not so bad vs. bad. A sin inside your mind is just as bad as if you acted on those thoughts. If you dream about or daydream about adultery, you are as guilty as if you committed adultery. IF you outwardly condemn folk for what you do in private, you have now added the sin of hypocrisy to your laundry list of hidden sin. Do not even attempt to convince yourself that God does not know about your sin. He does. Seek forgiveness, repent and guard your eye and ear gates. (Proverbs 28:13) If you are hooked on porn, throw it all out, block it on the internet and stay away from adult bookstores. If you are fornicating, just say no and find ways to redirect your energies. If you are lying, guard your heart and your mouth. If you are murdering folk with your mouth or your mind, pray before you speak and stay away from the people who trigger this response. And lastly, make certain you don't walk the same path mentally or put yourself back into the same compromising situations that lead to the secret sin.

Day 23

Getting Better!

14 I will be found by you, says the Lord, and I will bring you back from your captivity; I will gather you from all the

nations and from all the places where I have driven
you, says the Lord, and I will bring you to the place
from which I cause you to be carried away captive.
Jeremiah 29:14

In this day and age, depending on the lifestyle that we lead, it
is not farfetched to think that we may go a whole day without
speaking to another human being; i.e., a live person. If this
were the case, the loneliness could become unbearable. That to
me is like a kind of exile. Everyone goes through a valley, a dry
place or a season of unhappiness. But be strong.

GOD'S DEFINITION OF GETTING BETTER MAY NOT BE YOUR
DEFINITION. He may be leading you somewhere. There will
inevitably be a testimony that comes from your test. Pass the
test. Trials and tribulations eventually lead to victory. Speak it
and prepare for Victory! You may not always be able to see the
end result. You may not always be able to see the strategy of
the Great Chess Master (God). But He is working it out for your
good.

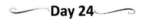Day 24

This Christmas Season

16 For God so loved the world that He gave His only begotten
Son, that whoever believes in Him should not perish
but have everlasting life.
John 3:16

There is joy at the birth of Jesus; however, we must understand
that God chose this route and became flesh, in order to
communicate with us. Jesus became a flesh and blood man
because He loves us; He came to bring truth and light in a world
of untruthful and dishonest men who cling to pagan rituals.

However, the most important reason He came was to be the ultimate sacrifice for our sins.

Essentially, God sacrificed one child to save His many others. We are His children; so as such, God gave us power and authority. (We tend to forget it; but it is the same power that raised Jesus from the dead and it is on the inside of you!)

So be careful not to make this season all about the light, glitz and glamor of a commercialized Christmas. Recognize and celebrate this season for the real reason.

Why are your rejoicing? How can you show the real meaning/spirit of Christmas this year?

_____
_____
_____
_____
_____
_____
_____
_____
_____
_____
_____
_____
_____
_____
_____
_____

Rejoice!

Day 25

This Christmas Season – Part 2

**16 For God so loved the world that He gave His only begotten
Son, that whoever believes in Him should not perish
but have everlasting life.
John 3:16**

God desired to cleanse us of the sinful nature, innate to
mankind; so Abba sent His Son to earth. God (Jesus) who was
righteous, blameless and divine lived in the midst of His
creations. Creations that were flawed, only because they were
born into sin. Creations that were profane, wicked, even those
who made themselves known as His enemies. Could you do it;
send your firstborn child to become The Prince of Peace/a living
sacrifice?

God loves us and He sends His blessings to show His affection.
Best of all, He sent us the gift of His Son to be our Savior and
Lord. Send God a gift this season—your contrite, repentant,
grateful heart—to show Him He has not loved in vain.

Day 26

Don't Let the Enemy Define Your Normal!

**5 Trust in the Lord with all your heart, And lean not on your
own understanding; 6 In all your ways acknowledge Him, And
He shall direct your paths.
Proverbs 3:5-6**

One of the easiest ways for the enemy to derail our destiny is
to cause us to act on something prematurely (lean to our own
understanding). We want what everyone else has, but it does

not always happen that way. Let's take the example of my own fertility. This is a tricky point to make; so bear with me.

God is a healer, as we have seen people healed time and again. I watched my own dad pray for women who wanted to conceive and they did. However, as young Christians, we have drilled into us that we should abstain from sex. As an unmarried adult woman, when faced with debilitating cycles, caused by fibroid tumors, I chose to have surgery.

Why? Because the pain was unbearable and the thought of having a child while unmarried was scandalous. (I am old school.) That overshadowed the possibility of praying for my healing and waiting to have the child when married. Rubbish you say? Yes. I convinced myself that I did not want to just "get pregnant without my child having a father," so that made it easier. Last, but not least, I got tired of being sick; that overshadowed everything else. I just wanted to be normal and finally it was within reach (the first trick of the enemy). See the truth is, I forgot who I was and I forgot what God is capable of doing; I settled for normal versus trusting God. As a child of the Most High, we should never just settle for normal.

 Day 27

Don't Let the Enemy Define Your Normal! — Part 2

5 Trust in the Lord with all your heart, And lean not on your own understanding; 6 In all your ways acknowledge Him, And He shall direct your paths.
Proverbs 3:5-6

My emotions ran the full gamut. I felt like my faith wasn't strong enough, like maybe I wasn't supposed to be married and have a child and like there was no hope for me to have a normal life. That was the second trick of the enemy. The enemy wanted me to stay in that self-imposed hole of despondency. He did not intend for me to bounce back.

Don't let the enemy define your normal. There were other options for me. I adopted and now have a highly discernable, strong, handsome, bundle of joy. That is the baby God gave me. God can replace everything that you have lost. Don't look at things in then natural. Use discernment and trust God.

—— Day 28 ——

Guilt, The Enemies' Secret Weapon

13 No temptation has overtaken you except such as is common to man; but God is faithful, who will not allow you to be tempted beyond what you are able, but with the temptation will also make the way of escape, that you may be able to bear it.
1 Corinthians 10:13

Guilt is a powerful tool of the enemy. For people who are plagued by self-condemnation about things they have been led of the flesh to do, guilt is probably at the root of the problem. There is something that they have done in their life that they feel guilty about. It may be something as simple as wasting time at work, or something more significant like fornication or cheating on a spouse. Guilt can be built on a web of lies or rooted in a single action. Are you plagued by guilt or self-condemnation? Think back, you have felt guilty about something for one of three reasons—you knew it was wrong, you liked it or you wanted to do it again.

In God's eyes, when it comes to sin, no one sin is greater than another. But since guilt is a human emotion, we can make distinctions about degrees of guilt. Acts 8:22 states, *repent therefore of this your wickedness, and pray God if perhaps the thought of your heart may be forgiven you.* Ask Him; God can and will have compassion on you and cast your sins into the pits of Hell. Just do not go back and wallow in the sin again.

Day 29

Guilt and Self-Condemnation

19 Now the works of the flesh are evident, which are: adultery, fornication, uncleanness, lewdness, 20 idolatry, sorcery, hatred, contentions, jealousies, outbursts of wrath, selfish ambitions, dissensions, heresies, 21 envy, murders, drunkenness, revelries, and the like; ... those who practice such things will not inherit the kingdom of God.
Galatians 5:19-21

Often we transfer the feelings associated with guilt to our relationships; however, sometimes the relationship itself can be the source of the guilt. If it gets bad enough, it can taint everything we touch. Don't allow guilt or shortsightedness to undermine your relationship; be it spiritual, physical, emotional or platonic. Know what you are getting into before you do it.

<u>Type of Relationship</u>	<u>Be Aware</u>
Spiritual **Relationships:**	Know whether it is God ordained or a distraction of the enemy. Above all, pray about them.
Physical Relationships:	Sometimes conversation is just as damaging as the physical act— the guilt can be just as deep. Don't sit on a high horse and say, "Well I never..."

Emotional Relationships: Are you supposed to have that deep abiding soul tie with that person? If a person's season has passed, pray, break that soul tie and let them go!

Platonic Relationships: If they bring more baggage to the RELATIONSHIP than even God can handle, you need to rethink your friendship, or at the very least, set some parameters.

Those right relationships will be fruitful and edify you, not tear you down. Today make a sincere effort to replace guilt, shame and regret with innocence, honor and happiness. Some relationships may need to be dissolved. Others may just need to be reevaluated and new parameters set. You must seek God about the situation; if need be, then repent, ask for His forgiveness and accept it; then forgive yourself.

 **Day 30**

Let It All Go

8 Above all, love each other deeply, because love covers over a multitude of sins.
1 Peter 4:8

Is it enough to love the Lord but still have a sour attitude? Is it enough to love the Lord without showing love to your fellow man? Sometimes we hear scuttlebutt about other Christians. You know the ones. Those who live one way in public and another way in private. (Side note: Secrets never truly remain secret; especially if another person is involved.)

We must not treat total strangers or frenemies better than we treat our spouse or kids. Your family must not suffer through the backlash of your transferred anger and frustrations with your life, job or mental anguish. If you are walking around with a bad attitude, it is bound to color the way you look at the world and react to situations. The family suffers because the "'tudes" have taken over. Attitudes come along, aptitude goes down, fortitude goes out the window and the Beatitudes are forgotten. We cannot get mad because things do not always go our way. Let. Things. Go.

What is causing you to step outside of your character? What do you need to let go today?

_____

_____

_____

_____

_____

⌒Day 31⌒

Let It All Go — Part 2

> 8 Above all, love each other deeply, because love covers over a multitude of sins.
> 1 Peter 4:8

You cannot truthfully say that you love God and do not have Agape or Phileo love for your fellow man. You cannot serve God with a hard heart. Ephesians 4:18 states, *they are darkened in their understanding, alienated from the life of God because of the ignorance that is in them, due to their hardness of heart.* Holding onto grudges, hate, apathy, or any sin will taint your praise. Ask God for His forgiveness, accept it and forgive yourself. Then, forgive those who have wronged you. Forgiveness is for you.

Sometime this New Year's Eve, find a quiet moment and pour your soul out to God. Allow Him to move on your heart. As He moves, all that hurt, bitterness and anger will melt away. Just make sure you do not hold onto a little bit of it. Don't take that baggage into the new year.

Embrace love. Embrace forgiveness. Let. It. All. Go.

January

By: Venus Griffin &
Shayla Donaldson

Day 1

Guarded By Peace
By: Venus Griffin

7 and the peace of God, which surpasses all understanding, will guard your hearts and minds through Christ Jesus.
Philippians 4:7

We are told of how Jesus and the disciples were on a ship, He fell asleep and a storm arose. They woke Him, asking if He really cared that they were in danger. Jesus' response is one that comes to mind when going through my personal storms and tests. "Oh Ye of little faith." They had seen Him perform many miracles and had not come to trust Him or truly know Him. That is shocking after He rebuked the wind, calmed the waters, and ended the storm. They even asked, "What manner of man is this that even the wind obeys him?"

Jesus is our Prince of Peace. He is the Peace of God which passes all understanding. Reading this scripture assures us that the peace of God shall keep us. The word keep means to guard or protect. This means that no matter what we face or how ferocious the storms, we are guarded by the peace of God. Rest in His ability to protect you. Are you fearful about hopes, dreams, or the future? Oh Ye of little faith. He that calms the storms and seas can quiet your weary soul. Set the tone for this year and TRUST HIM!

WHEN WE PUT
OUR PROBLEMS IN
GOD'S HANDS,
HE PUTS HIS PEACE IN
OUR HEARTS.

Day 2

A Great Resource/Source For Any Issue
By: Shayla Donaldson

**105 Your word is a lamp to my feet And a light
to my path.
Psalm 119:105**

I love that I can go to the Word of God for any issue; there is a scripture to help me work through it. And there are so many resources at my fingertips. I really have no excuse not to go to the Scripture for encouragement, motivation or even just help with an issue. I love the feel of my actual Bible; so I can have something in my hand and be able to highlight the scriptures I read and take notes. But if I'm in a hurry or if I just need a "quick fix" I can Google a verse on my phone or do a thorough search while at work sitting at my desk. Through the miracle of technology, I can even pull up my Bible app on my tablet to look up scriptures that are relevant to my needs in that moment. I'm never surprised at how God can speak to me in the simplest way. He never ceases to amaze me! Know that God is not so big or far away that we can't reach Him when we need Him!

Day 3

The Grace of God
By: Venus Griffin

**7 But what things were gain to me, these I have counted loss
for Christ. 8 Yet indeed I also count all things loss for the
excellence of the knowledge of Christ Jesus my Lord, for whom
I have suffered the loss of all things, and count them as
rubbish, that I may gain Christ 9 and be found in Him, not
having my own righteousness, which is from the law, but that**

which is through faith in Christ, the righteousness which is
from God by faith;
Philippians 3:7-9

Sometimes in life we misunderstand the grace of God; what He does for us even though we don't deserve it. Then we take advantage of the mercy of God; how He guards us from what we do deserve. It is the enemy's job to make us feel accomplished, successful and "blessed" even though we KNOW that we are outside of the Will of God. We must not allow the increase of money; material gain or even education to make us feel that God is pleased with us. Don't be deceived! Without Christ, all of these things amount to NOTHING!!

Too often we believe material things have value, but we must consider them worthless because of what Christ has done. Yes, everything else is worthless when compared with the infinite value of knowing Christ Jesus my Lord. For His sake discard everything else, counting it all as garbage, so that you can gain Christ and become one with Him. It is worth the effort.

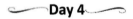Day 4

Life Is Short
By: Shayla Donaldson

47 Remember how short my time is; For what futility
have You created all the children of men?
Psalm 89:47

If you knew today was your last day here on Earth what would you do? What would you do differently? How would you treat people? What would you try to accomplish? Where would you go? Who would you talk to? Who would you forgive? Who would you ask forgiveness from? Where would you make preparations to go? Would you be afraid or calm?

Of course we will never know when our last day is but we should live like every day or moment we have could very well be. Time is advancing; it doesn't stop for anyone and life is short. I believe James 4:14 refers to it as a vapor. We are all only here for a brief time. Let's not waste it on unnecessary worries or things that don't really matter. Instead let's wisely choose to embrace the fullness of our purpose and assignment given to us by God!

Day 5

Purpose And Passion
By: Shayla Donaldson

11 For I know the thoughts that I think toward you, says the Lord, thoughts of peace and not of evil, to give you a future and a hope.
Jeremiah 29:11

Pray this today: *Lord, let nothing hinder me from my purpose and passion today! Let me fully engage in who I am in You and what You have called and chosen me to do today. May You be pleased and glorified above all! May lives be touched and souls saved because they have seen Your light and love in me, in Jesus' Name! Amen!*

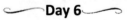Day 6

Pray Continually
By: Venus Griffin

17 pray without ceasing,
1 Thessalonians 5:17

At the end of last year, everyone was reflecting on the past year and making resolutions for the new year. As Christians, one of the goals that always makes the resolution list is the need spend more time in prayer. So like all other resolutions, we start out strong, setting a specific time each day to communicate with our Heavenly Father. But as time passes, we become too busy for whatever reason to keep those prayer-time appointments and we end up making the same resolution every year because we failed to follow through. Well this year let's take a different approach. It is day six, don't slack up!

Our prayer life should not just be a time we set aside daily to tell God about our problems. Prayer is a two-way line of communication between you and God. You talk to Him and He talks back; He talks to you and you talk back. Because God is not confined by time, He does not choose a specific time of day to speak. He keeps the line of communication open all throughout the day and night, speaking to and guiding us. Whether you are asking Him for help or thanking Him for a blessing, there will be plenty of opportunities to speak to Abba today; don't overlook them in the hustle and bustle of life.

Pray Regardless! **Thaddeus Miles Photography**

Day 7

Take Me Back to Where I First Believed
By: Venus Griffin

1 Moreover the word of the Lord came to me, saying, 2 "Go and cry in the hearing of Jerusalem, saying, 'Thus says the Lord: "I remember you, The kindness of your youth, The love of your betrothal, When you went after Me in the wilderness, In a land not sown.
Jeremiah 2: 1-2

Take a moment and think back to the day that you decided to give your life to Christ. Oh what a marvelous day it was; one that would stay etched in your memory for a lifetime. I can remember the spiritual euphoria that overtook me as I said "YES," to God. I didn't have a full understanding of what to expect next, but I knew that I wanted to fully give myself to this relationship. Nothing else in life mattered; not the troubles that I faced at home, the sickness in my body, the struggles in my mind, my financial situation, or my status in society. None of that mattered, because I had just become one with the solution to every problem and issue that concerned me: Jesus. I had no worries and I had no reason to stress about anything because I was on fire for God and He was the answer to it all. I would wake up reading His word and fall asleep the same way. Time to spend in prayer and worship was never something that I had to find; I intentionally made time daily for those things. I went out of my way to show and prove my devotion to Him with my actions and my lifestyle. I didn't just expect Him to "know my heart."

But as life continued its forward march and I began to encounter people, things and situations, that euphoria slowly drifted to just a mundane, uninvolved relationship of "hello" and "goodbye" with the God I was once passionate about.

It is very easy to become common with God when life seems to be having its way with you, but today I invite you back to the place where you first believed. I invite you back to the peace and joy that you had in just knowing that you were free from the yoke of bondage and free to live again! I invite you into the knowledge that many are the afflictions of the righteous but you can rest in the fact that God always comes to your rescue (Psalm 34:19). I invite you to place your focus back on the one who has offered to carry every burden and help in every situation. I invite you to fall for Jesus all over again, but this time with a greater love, greater understanding, greater patience, greater commitment and greater maturity. Welcome back to the place where you first believed.

 Day 8

Search Me Lord
By: Shayla Donaldson

2 Examine me, O LORD, and prove me; Try my mind and my heart. For Your lovingkindness is before my eyes.
Psalm 26:2

Salvation is not a destination. It is the beginning of a journey that we must consciously choose to walk each and every day. We must wake up with a mindset that we are going to allow God to take the lead in our thinking, our talking and our behavior. And we must continuously ask God to evaluate our hearts and minds, because if we are honest there is always something that needs repair, fixing or correcting. It's certainly not easy and most of the time we don't even want to know what areas in our life need improving. Why? Because it challenges the idea that we are 'perfect' and 'have it all together'. But God knows and sees all. He sees that is not like Him; every imperfection, issue, thought, action, insecurity, etc. So there is no sense in trying to hide it from Him.

Day 9

Search Me Lord — Part 2
By: Shayla Donaldson

2 Examine me, O LORD, and prove me; Try my mind and my heart. For Your lovingkindness is before my eyes.
Psalm 26:2

We should just allow the Word to begin a transformation in us from the inside out. It starts with us acknowledging and inviting Him to examine us according to His standard, which is the Word of God. We will never achieve perfection in our flesh and we can only strive to achieve spiritual perfection through Jesus Christ.

Today, my prayer is that each of us will take this opportunity to invite God into our heart and mind and ask Him to search and examine us. Give Him free access to our thoughts, words and actions and let Him lovingly show us the areas that need more of Him.

Pray this today: *Lord, search us today and every day! Search every corner and crevice. You know us better than we know ourselves. Search even the places we try to hide from You and try to ignore. Remove any and everything that is not like You. Fill us with Your Spirit until we overflow. Let us be overtaken by spiritual things, in Jesus' Name! Amen.*

Day 10

Seasons Change
By: Shayla Donaldson

22 While the earth remains, seedtime and harvest, cold and heat, winter and summer, and day and night shall not cease.
Genesis 8:22

Have you ever looked back over the last year of your life? The last five or ten years? Isn't it amazing how different things have become in such short periods of time? For most of us, hopefully we have grown and matured into much wiser and smarter versions of our younger selves.

Some of us have probably experienced minor changes or transitions, such as moving into a new home or starting a new job. And others of us have probably experienced some pretty major changes, such as losing a job, the death of a loved one, a divorce or the end of a relationship with a close friend. Sometimes it's easier to adjust than not. To be perfectly honest, most people would prefer to remain in their comfortable box with the same friends, job, routine, etc., forever.

The reality is change is inevitable; our lives will constantly evolve. Even though it is often very difficult to process the changes that will take place and understand the "why" associated with these changes, we have to trust that the transitions and experiences we encounter will make us better and not worse when we put them in God's hands.

Today, remember that seasons will change but we must not be afraid to trust His <u>plan</u> and go with His <u>flow</u>.

TrustGod

Day 11

Jesus At The Center
By: Venus Griffin

33 But seek first the kingdom of God and His righteousness, and all these things shall be added to you.
Matthew 6:33

In today's society, we can get sucked into the hype of "living life to the fullest." The world goads us to seek fulfillment for our lives. We have career goals, education, family, relationships, houses, cars, social status, fashion and the trendiest this and that! Now there is nothing wrong with having some of these things. The problem comes when we make these things our focus, and it's unfortunate that many of us have done just that.

The amazing thing about a Christ-centered life is the harvest that we receive as we focus on Him. He promises to provide everything we need and even those things for an abundant life. So in your daily pursuit of life, liberty and happiness, remember to keep your motives pure and Christ as your focus (Proverbs 16:3). From this point flows every great thing imaginable in life!

Knowing Jesus   Thaddeus Miles Photography

Day 12

Moving Forward
By: Shayla Donaldson

12 Not that I have already attained, or am already perfected; but I press on, that I may lay hold of that for which Christ Jesus has also laid hold of me. 13 Brethren, I do not count myself to have apprehended; but one thing I do, forgetting those things which are behind and reaching forward to those things which are ahead, 14 I press toward the goal for the prize of the upward call of God in Christ Jesus.
Philippians 3:12-14

Often, we are our own worst enemy. We make it hard for our own progress and growth because we are mentally bound by past mistakes. We allow the enemy to convince us that our past is so horrible and messed up that we will never be worthy of God's grace and love. And the truth is—the devil is somewhat right. But what he's wrong about is God's unconditional love and grace toward us. In our own strength and power, we will never be worthy enough to earn God's love and forgiveness. It is just not possible to achieve in our flesh. However, once we accept Christ and become new creatures in Him (2 Corinthians 5:17), our past mistakes are erased and we are made over into new beings that are patterned, shaped and molded in the likeness of Christ!

There is no need for us to dwell in our past mistakes and get bogged down in the weight of things that we can't go back and change anyway. We must press toward things which are ahead. If we are in Christ, that means we are pressing toward spiritual things and a new beginning. We are now on a journey to become more like Christ and the experiences we encounter along this journey will begin to develop us into Christ-like beings with a mind, heart and soul to serve Him in spirit and truth. We must start today and embrace a fresh start and purpose within our self to let go of everything and anything that is hindering us from moving forward in Christ!

As you go through your day, keep these tips at the forefront of your heart and mind:

- Forgive yourself and others
- Release bitterness, anger and resentment
- Free your mind of anything that is not like Christ!

Day 13

Boldness To Proclaim
By: Shayla Donaldson

12 ...in whom we have boldness and access with confidence through faith in Him.
Ephesians 3:12

How many of us refrain from witnessing or water down our message out of fear that something we say will offend or out of fear that our beliefs will be challenged or contested? Surely the world around us is changing but the Gospel is not and never will; neither should our faith or willingness to share it.

Pray this today: *Lord, let me be bold and courageous enough to proclaim the Gospel whenever and wherever the opportunities present. Let me speak Your Word with clarity and conviction instead of fear or shame. Even in the face of fear and/or persecution let me stand firm in my belief that Jesus Christ is Lord and reigns supreme in my life, in Jesus' Name! Amen!*

Day 14

Power To Declare And Decree
By: Shayla Donaldson

28 You will also declare a thing And it will be established for you; So light will shine on your ways.

Job 22:28

Your words have power! What you decree and declare in His Name shall be established according to His Will. Today is all about prayer!

Pray this today: *Lord, I pray that the words I speak on this day will give life and peace. I pray that I rely on the Holy Spirit to choose my words more carefully and consciously instead of reacting or responding according to my flesh or feelings. I want my words to encourage and empower instead of tear down and hold back. I want my words to proclaim Your goodness and glory everywhere my feet touch. I believe it is so in Jesus' Name! Amen!*

Day 15

Live In TRUTH!
By: Shayla Donaldson

17 For the flesh lusts against the Spirit, and the Spirit against the flesh; and these are contrary to one another, so that you do not do the things that you wish.

Galatians 5:17

As much as I love God and strive to serve, honor and obey Him every day, I still struggle with discouragement, fear, doubt, anxiety, worry, etc. It's not because I don't know Him or because I don't love Him but it's because there is a battle going on between my mind and spirit, every single day. My spirit wants to fulfill the things of God, but my mind wants to fulfill the things of the flesh. My spirit wants to believe the promises of God but my mind wants to believe what is logical and makes sense.

So every day, I must remind myself of God's Word and His promises and speak them over my life. The enemy knows that if he can distract, discourage or convince me that what God says is not true or going to happen, he can get me completely off track and out of sync with God. But I refuse to believe what the devil says! He is a LIAR and there is absolutely NO truth in him whatsoever! I believe God! He is the TRUTH.

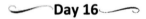 Day 16

Live For Today
By: Shayla Donaldson

34 Therefore do not worry about tomorrow, for tomorrow will worry about its own things. Sufficient for the day is its own trouble.
Matthew 6:34

Sometimes we get so burdened down thinking about tomorrow or next week or next year and we allow the pressure of unrealistic expectations to discourage us from moving forward. Listen, we can't do it all. There are some things we have to take in small chunks and others, we have to attempt several times before we get it right. That's ok. God is patient with us as long as we are striving for righteousness through Him daily. So just put one foot in front of the other; one step at a time. Have a blessed day!

Day 17

Maintaining Focus While Walking On Water

By: Venus Griffin

22 Immediately Jesus made His disciples get into the boat and go before Him to the other side, while He sent the multitudes away. 23 And when He had sent the multitudes away, He went up on the mountain by Himself to pray. Now when evening came, He was alone there. 24 But the boat was now in the middle of the sea, tossed by the waves, for the wind was contrary. 25 Now in the fourth watch of the night Jesus went to them, walking on the sea. 26 And when the disciples saw Him walking on the sea, they were troubled, saying, "It is a ghost!" And they cried out for fear. 27 But immediately Jesus spoke to them, saying, "Be of good cheer! It is I; do not be afraid." 28 And Peter answered Him and said, "Lord, if it is You, command me to come to You on the water." 29 So He said, "Come." And when Peter had come down out of the boat, he walked on the water to go to Jesus. 30 But when he saw that the wind was boisterous, he was afraid; and beginning to sink he cried out, saying, "Lord, save me!" 31 And immediately Jesus stretched out His hand and caught him, and said to him, "O you of little faith, why did you doubt?" 32 And when they got into the boat, the wind ceased. 33 Then those who were in the boat came and worshiped Him, saying, "Truly You are the Son of God."

Matthew 14:22-33

Many of us are just like Peter. We have dreams and goals that we want to accomplish. We've fasted, prayed and sought God about it and after we receive that *yes* in our spirit, we move forward with great faith and confidence, with our eyes on the prize. Then in the midst of stepping out and trusting God, distractions show up and we take our focus off of the promise.

We forget that we were granted permission to walk on water. Distractions come in so many different forms and they are inevitable, as we take this journey with Christ. We must not become fearful or discouraged to the point of giving up! If you find yourself in that place, follow Peter's lead, and quickly remember where your help comes from. Examine your life today and find those areas that you've allowed to sink because you lost your focus. Oh ye of little faith, why did you doubt?

What are you doubting God about today?

_____
_____
_____
_____
_____
_____
_____
_____

Day 18

Don't Be Deceived
By: Shayla Donaldson

5 ...casting down arguments and every high thing that exalts itself against the knowledge of God, bringing every thought into captivity to the obedience of Christ...
2 Corinthians 10:5

If we rely on our emotions, we will be taken on a constant roller coaster of feelings and thoughts that are contrary to the Word of God. The enemy sees every thought and emotion we have and he patiently waits for us; so that he can attack every good thing we decree and declare. It is his objective to discourage us from believing that God's Promises are possible for us. He ensures that we pay close attention to those around us that are experiencing God's blessings and then points us right back to our own situation to remind us of what hasn't happened yet for us. Don't be deceived!

Cast down every negative thought, every thought that is contrary to what God has said. The enemy knows that if he can get our focus on what hasn't taken place, then we will begin to doubt what God has purposed to do for us. We will block our own blessings by not believing that it will happen. The sad thing is when this happens, we are usually right on the verge of receiving the breakthrough! Stand on God's Word! Stand on His Promises! Draw closer to God and rebuke the devil! God's got it covered!

Day 19

Finding The Good In The Bad
By: Venus Griffin

71 It is good for me that I have been afflicted,
That I may learn Your statutes.
Psalm 119:71

Life is full of surprises. At times it appears, we are riding an emotional roller coaster of ups, downs, ins and outs. We have to learn to balance crying with celebrating, pain with praise, and soaring with sorrow. And in dealing with such a conundrum of things it becomes difficult to find the good in the bad.

Psalms 119:71 helps us to realize that even "bad things" serve good purposes. To afflict is to cause pain, to torture, or add sorrow. It would seem that nothing good could come out of being tortured or being pained. However, the psalmist finds peace and tranquility because he shifts his focus from the problems associated with the affliction, to the purpose of the affliction.

Name five things that you considered bad that have happened to you.

_____

_____

_____

_____

_____

— Day 20 —

Finding The Good In The Bad — Part 2
By: Venus Griffin

> 71 It is good for me that I have been afflicted,
> That I may learn Your statutes.
> Psalm 119:71

The writer recognizes that the nature of affliction is that it is permitted by God, because it teaches us invaluable lessons about who He is and what He expects of us. David acknowledges affliction as a teacher and he has become a student learning about his God. His resolve was this; "IT WAS GOOD FOR ME THAT I HAVE BEEN AFFLICTED..." Considering all of the bad things he had endured, he managed to find the good in them.

Perhaps you don't understand why you're going through a particular situation right now; perhaps you can't find the good in a bad situation. Do what David did; stop focusing on the pain of your story and start searching for the purpose.

Romans 8:28 states, *and we know that all things work together for good to them that love God, to them who are the called according to his purpose.*

Now List the positive things that happened as a result of the bad things.

_____

_____

_____

_____

_____

Day 21

Prayer For Families
By: Shayla Donaldson

15 And if it seems evil to you to serve the LORD, choose for yourselves this day whom you will serve... But as for me and my house, we will serve the LORD.
Joshua 24:15

Pray this today: Lord, *You know every situation and every need. Cover and protect families, heal broken hearts, damaged relationships, restore love, peace and joy where it may be absent. Fill voids left by hurt, pain, confusion and death. Renew hearts and minds. Open eyes to be able to see the attacks of the enemy. Give strength and courage to stand and fight. Meet every need. Heal sickness and disease. Repair where abuse has shattered. Build up where lies and discouragement have torn down. Allow Your Word and Spirit to become alive and active; so we can destroy every trick, antic and dart the enemy throws. Embrace us in love and wrap us in Your tender grace and mercy, in Jesus' Name! Amen!*

Family Comes In All Shapes and Sizes
Thaddeus Miles Photography

Day 22

I'm Not A Superhero!

By: Shayla Donaldson

25 Therefore I say to you, do not worry about your life, what you will eat or what you will drink; nor about your body, what you will put on. Is not life more than food and the body more than clothing?

Matthew 6:25

I am naturally a planner. I have more calendars and task lists than I know what to do with. But often as I begin to plan out my week it seems like my to-do list is never ending. There is just so much to do and certainly not enough time to do it. This usually makes me frustrated and stressed. But, as always when I get frustrated and overwhelmed, the Spirit of the Lord reminds me not to stress about things outside of my current time space. He gently reminds to do what I can now and leave the rest to its own day and time. So, today I choose to remember that I'm not superwoman and I can't do everything at the snap of my fingers. I can only take it one bit at a time until it gets done. Have a blessed day and enjoy your NOW!

⌒Day 23⌒

Picture Day
By: Shayla Donaldson

> 28 And we know that all things work together for good to those who love God, to those who are the called according to His purpose.
> Romans 8:28

I remember a few months ago when my daughter's school pictures came. I beamed with pride as I looked at her sweet but awkward smile on her first set of school pictures. A chuckle escaped me as I thought about that morning and all that occurred. It was CRAZY! I had woken up late, she didn't want to get up and it seemed like I was rushing but getting absolutely nowhere. I remember being flustered, frustrated and tired. But as I looked at the proofs I didn't see any signs of the drama that happened on that day. All I could see was a happy and excited little girl, who I can imagine was probably saying "cheese" as she smiled big for the cameras.

Isn't it funny how things happen in our life and in that very moment the tension, worry and frustration consumes us. We get weighed down and burdened and sometimes think "How in the world am I going to make it past this situation or issue?" But as the days, weeks, months, and years go by we look back on that situation and realize it really wasn't that bad and that even though we didn't think we would make it, guess what? WE SURVIVED! And we did it with a smile, albeit an awkward one, but a smile nonetheless. Have a blessed day and stay encouraged!

**Day 24**

Defeat Discouragement With The Word
By: Shayla Donaldson

1 Therefore, since we are surrounded by such a great cloud of witnesses, let us throw off everything that hinders and the sin that so easily entangles. And let us run with perseverance the race marked out for us.
Hebrews 12:1

Recently I was dealing with a situation and began to feel a little discouraged, almost to the point of defeat about a particular situation. But as I begin to pray about it, the Spirit brought this scripture to mind. I was reminded to lay aside every burden, weight and hindrance and to continue moving forward on the path God has set for me. I wrote the following prayer in my journal. I pray this encourages you.

Pray this today: *Lord, I feel stagnant and stuck. I feel weighed down with the pressures of life, the burden of high expectations and overwhelming responsibilities. I ask that You rid me of this baggage and weight that is holding me down or keeping me from moving forward or higher in You. I believe it and declare it is so, in Jesus' Name. Amen!*

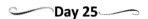**Day 25**

The Struggle Will Abate
By: Venus Griffin

19 For this is commendable, if because of conscience toward God one endures grief, suffering wrongfully. 20 For what credit is it if, when you are beaten for your faults, you take it patiently? But when you do good and suffer, if you take it

patiently, this is commendable before God. 21 For to this you were called, because Christ also suffered for us, leaving us an example, that you should follow His steps:
1Peter 2:19-21

There was a point in my life when I didn't understand why I was suffering, even though I was striving to live all that I knew through God's word. It seemed like everything had fallen apart since I had made up my mind to get it together. As I studied my word, it didn't take long for me to come across and find encouragement in the scriptures. For it is commendable if someone bears up under the pain of unjust suffering because they are conscious of God. But how is it to your credit if you receive a beating for doing wrong and endure it? But if you suffer for doing good and you endure it, *this is commendable before God. To this you were called, because Christ suffered for you, leaving you an example, that you should follow in His steps.* (1 Peter 2:19-21) People may try to label your unjust suffering as punishment for what you've done wrong, but endure anyway! The struggle will eventually abate. God commends you!

Day 26

Cleaning Season
By: Venus Griffin

5 For those who live according to the flesh set their minds on the things of the flesh, but those who live according to the Spirit, the things of the Spirit. 6 For to be carnally minded is death, but to be spiritually minded is life and peace. 7 Because the carnal mind is enmity against God; for it is not subject to the law of God, nor indeed can be. 8 So then, those who are in the flesh cannot please God.
Romans 8:5-8

I know that we normally wait until the Spring, but let's just make this the beginning of cleaning season. I chose this season because it may take a little while to sift through the closet of our lives and identify and then discard feelings and ideas. You know, those areas where we have allowed our flesh to dominate. Today is a great day to take a looong look in the mirror and decide to be REAL with yourself and with God; it's just between you and Him. The easy part is that God already knows; so before you open that closet door, pray that God opens your eyes to identify areas where your flesh prevails. Then pray that He humbles you enough to yield to the power of Holy Spirit, who gives you the strength to say goodbye to those things; never to have them return again.

The bible gives us a clear guideline to help us recognize that which is of the Spirit and that which is of the flesh (Galatians 5:17-25). Where have you set your mind; what has your attention, and on what is your concentration focused? Is your focus on things of the spirit or that of the flesh?

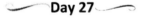 **Day 27**

Spiritual Closet Cleaning
By: Shayla Donaldson

**10 Create in me a clean heart, O God, And renew a
steadfast spirit within me.
Psalm 51:10**

Have you already done your spiritual closet cleaning yet? If you are anything like me, I always use the approaching New Year as an opportunity to do some good cleaning. I begin pulling things out of my closets that I haven't worn or been able to wear in years. If not, let's get started. Start trying on things to see what still fits and what's still "in style." Then we will create a pile to throw away and a pile that can be repurposed or changed. In the same way that we go through our natural closet, we should take the time to clean out our spiritual closet.

Here are a few steps that I think would be great for cleaning out your spiritual closet:

1. Clean out old and worn out attitudes.
2. Clean out hidden corners and crevices and release anything you are secretly hoarding.
3. Dust off those "religious" traditions and rid yourself of thought patterns that are no longer working.
4. Get rid of those burdens that are weighing you down and holding you back.
5. Make room for new, improved and better.
6. Replace "old" with "refreshed" and "renewed".
7. Stock up on spiritual attributes for the new season (peace, joy, love, etc.)

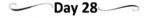 Day 28

God Will Not Put More On You Than You Can Bear
By: Venus Griffin

22 Cast your burden on the Lord, And He shall sustain you; He shall never permit the righteous to be moved.
Psalm 55:22

This is a real *cute* statement that we like to throw out when facing hard times in life; but it can't be found anywhere in the bible. It's not a statement that I use and it doesn't encourage me, simply because it places the emphasis on me and what I can bear. The truth is that in this life there WILL be times when burdens are too much for us to bear and it is clear that our strength will surely fail us at some point or another; I've been there many times. I found those times of weakness, when trials and sufferings are much more than I can bear, to be a be a reason to turn to God; to allow him to work and handle the situation. I could not do it in my own strength.

The bible tells us to cast our cares upon the Lord and He will sustain us. To cast means to throw or to fling. So when life brings a heavy burden, we need not waste time trying to carry it on our own. The little strength that we have should only be used in the casting process.

What do you need to cast onto God's shoulders today?

_____
_____
_____
_____
_____

Day 29

God Will Not Put More On You Than You Can Bear
Part 2
By: Venus Griffin

22 Cast your burden on the Lord, And He shall sustain you; He shall never permit the righteous to be moved.
Psalm 55:22

God cares for His people and He has given us a drop-off location for our burdens; it's too much for you, so give it to Him! And with that, He's also declared that He will never allow the righteous to be shaken, moved nor torn down. So if you ever find yourself in a moment or season where you feel like life is too much, you're going to lose your mind or you just want to throw in the towel, stop and take a self-evaluation: What is it that has me in this place? Am I casting or am I carrying?

I read this quote that blessed my life: "Our faithfulness is not demonstrated by how easily we are able to bear the burdens that come our way. Our faith is demonstrated by our recognition that we cannot bear the burdens ourselves and trust in the grace of God who bears them with us." (Unknown Quote) When you are weak, He is strong. Your strength will NOT always sustain you; but the Lord WILL. He's just waiting on you to cast it.

Day 30

Share the Struggle, Share the Victory
By: Shayla Donaldson

8 Therefore do not be ashamed of the testimony of our Lord, nor of me His prisoner, but share with me in the sufferings for the gospel according to the power of God,
2 Timothy 1:8

I don't know many people, if any that can stand flat footed in the face of disappointment, hurt, rejection or failure and still have a smile on their face or joy in their heart. If you have experienced true disappointment, you know how hard it is to keep from breaking down and giving up completely. It's a fight, literally, to keep it together. But somehow we muster up the strength to get up and get moving and eventually we realize that God has done what only He can do: worked it out! That's why it's so important that we be willing to share our struggle. Don't get me wrong, there is nothing easy about being honest and transparent and most people don't appreciate all that we have endured physically, mentally, emotionally and spiritually to even have a testimony to share. But there is a joy that comes in knowing that our struggles, experiences, trials, tribulations, pains and hurts are not all about us.

It may not seem like much while we are going through, but how amazing is it that God can use our messy situation to bless someone else and give them hope! As we learn what God would have us to learn from our situation, we are also being used by Him to teach others a powerful lesson, we must be the voice of assurance and reassurance that "yes God still loves us," "yes He still cares" and "yes He still holds our best interest at heart." Don't be afraid to let others know what God has brought you out of and certainly what He's bringing you through! In sharing our struggles, we not only give encouragement to those that need to be reminded of His mighty power but we are reminded of His victories in the midst of our hopeless situations!

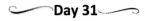 Day 31

Candy Confession
By: Shayla Donaldson

17 Therefore, to him who knows to do good and does not
do it, to him it is sin.
James 4:17

Ok, I must make an honest confession: I messed up! That's right I messed up and had to repent. So here's what happened: I was walking through a local craft store and as I proceeded to check out, I grabbed a bag of my favorite candy. I paid for it along with a few other items I needed that day. Within five minutes, I had eaten more than half the bag. You are probably wondering what could be so wrong about enjoying one of my favorite treats. Well, this was the day that my accountability partner and I had set aside every week to fast. We would check in with each other several times during the day and encourage each other through the hunger pains and tempting moments. I can't say I forgot because that would be untrue. As a matter of fact, my friend and I had just checked in with a simple text, "You still hanging in there?" So no, I didn't forget. I just saw the bag of candy and decided that I wanted it; even though I knew it was our day to fast.

Looking back, it seems a little weird to make such a big deal about a bag of candy. I'm sure God has no issue with me enjoying my favorite candy. But He absolutely does have a problem with me making commitments and not following through with them, especially those that are intended to honor Him. According to the Word of God, when we intentionally know to do something that is good and honorable and we do not, we have sinned. That seems so harsh to think about something so trivial in that way. But we must be careful to do what we know is right no matter how small or minor it may seem. God honors our commitments to Him and expects us to live righteous in all areas of our life; so choose wisely to do that today!

February

By: Nicole Peeples

～Day 1～

The Spirit Of Excellence

**23 And whatever you do, do it heartily,
as to the Lord and not to men.
Colossians 3:23**

Excellence is a reputation and so is mediocrity. Excellence is examining ourselves to determine the areas that need improvement. We should always ask ourselves, "How can what I'm doing, be done better?" It does not matter how trivial you deem your work. Sometimes we operate so long in mediocrity that we end up not being effective.

Striving for excellence helps fulfill the potential that God has placed inside of you. So, today, measure whatever you do, whether it be on your job, at church, or home; the question should be HOW can I improve this? I think we would soon find; we don't have much time to focus on others!

_____
_____
_____
_____
_____

～Day 2～

How To Recognize Satan's Lies

**5 casting down arguments and every high thing that exalts
itself against the knowledge of God, bringing every thought
into captivity to the obedience of Christ,
2 Corinthians 10:5**

Satan's job is to kill, steal, and destroy. We must recognize these lame, but consistent tactics; however, most times we don't. Satan knows all about our struggles and weaknesses. He knows what pushes our buttons. Use this as a great method of dispelling the lies that satan spews. Whatever thought that comes to mind, end it with "in Jesus' name." If it doesn't fit, then it's a lie. Example: I'm a failure, "in Jesus name" or I can do all things through Christ, "in Jesus' name." Which one is a lie? Make every thought OBEDIENT to Christ; i.e., The Word!

Day 3

How To Recognize Satan's Lies — Part 2

5 casting down arguments and every high thing that exalts itself against the knowledge of God, bringing every thought into captivity to the obedience of Christ,
2 Corinthians 10:5

Personally speaking, it seems that the moment you begin to walk in faith, the enemy comes in to attack the foundation of your beliefs. But, it is his job to do so. That's why we can never let him in the door or gate of our thoughts. I remember when I purchased my home in a subdivision in South Carolina years ago, all kind of people would drop by to pitch a sale; vacuum cleaners, alarms, cable, etc. I made the mistake of letting a Kirby vacuum cleaner salesman in the door. Two hours later, I was buying a Kirby!! Ugh. I didn't even want one, but she was so persistent and would not take no for an answer. Every excuse I gave, she had a remedy for it. She wore me down. Needless to say, after that, I stopped every sales person at the door! That's the same way we need to treat satan and his bag of tricks and lies. Stop him at the threshold of our minds. Layer by layer, he adds on to the lies until it has built walls that imprison us—strongholds! We become enslaved.

Today, focus on the Word to attack every lie as soon as it enters your mind. Don't let satan make you a slave to your negative thoughts!

_____

_____

_____

_____

_____

Day 4

Get Your Life!

28 Come to Me, all you who labor and are heavy laden, and I will give you rest. 29 Take My yoke upon you and learn from Me, for I am gentle and lowly in heart, and you will find rest for your souls. 30 For My yoke is easy and My burden is light.
Matthew 11:28-30

Sometimes we feel overwhelmed with all of the "things to do." It seems like at the time I cross one thing off my list, three more need to be added. I realize that in my own strength, I get aggravated and frustrated. Especially when I don't take the time to seek Him and His strength because I'm constantly in motion. But when I take the time to stop, meditate, read His Word, and listen to Him, He gives me a refreshing to do what I need to do in His grace.

Today, rest in His strength. He's waiting to endow us with it. Amidst your daily tasks, take a moment and seek Him.

Day 5

Fitly Joined Together

16 ...from whom the whole body, joined and knit together by what every joint supplies, according to the effective working by which every part does its share, causes growth of the body for the edifying of itself in love.

Ephesians 4:16

The world has evolved; human interaction has been significantly reduced. Think how frequently you get an operator instead of a live person whenever you call a company. Think about how there are more ATM's than ever before; so there's no need to go to the bank and see a person. Let's examine the banking network. Now, some accounts are free, as long as all transactions are done via the Internet or ATM. In fact, they penalize and charge you, if you visit the bank and interact with the teller. With this evolution, we become insensitive to human interaction. But, God created us to need each other. He created us with such unique qualities and characteristics, that we need each other to really be effective in building His kingdom. Sadly, we forget this easily.

How do I figure this? Because we operate in our self-sufficiency, because "we don't want others in our business." Also, because we have unresolved issues with others, and strained relationships. But it shows Spiritual maturity when we learn to depend on others and offer our unique abilities to each other.

Day 6

Contentment

9 The things which you learned and received and heard and saw in me, these do, and the God of

> peace will be with you...13 I can do all things
> through Christ who strengthens me.
> Philippians 4:9-13

The secret to contentment is to fully put our trust and confidence in God. We should learn to be at peace with the One who is omniscient, all knowing. He knows all about every aspect of our lives and we must trust Him to know that He will make every piece of our puzzled lives fit together perfectly. He cares for us just that much. I remember going through a range of emotions during my divorce, feeling as if I had lost everything—materially and emotionally. I felt like my life had been broken into a million pieces. But, there was one thing that I remembered and it stuck with me, as I talked to my dad that day about how I was feeling. I can hear these words, "You must know that God will never allow you to go through anything and not make something good come out of it. He's not that type of God. Don't worry about what you have lost, He has better for you." And those words were so very true. I've learned so many valuable lessons through it all, have regained a strength that I didn't even know I had, recovered what I've lost and more. The list goes on and on. I'm getting happy just thinking about it all! Learn to be content in whatever you are experiencing, knowing that God has a plan just for you!

Are you content? How can you reach contentment in your life?

_____

_____

_____

_____

_____

_____

_____

_____

Day 7

Contentment — Part 2

9 The things which you learned and received and heard and saw in me, these do, and the God of peace will be with you...13 I can do all things through Christ who strengthens me.
Philippians 4:9-13

The next step to living in contentment is to be obedient to His Word. We must practice the precepts of God. When we choose Christ to come into our lives, we are now under "new management;" the management of Jesus Christ. He will direct our lives, but only if we allow Him to do so. When we obey Him, we choose to be covered under all His promises and we give Him the freedom to work through and in us. This gives us a peace in our heart! Today, be at peace with God's work in your life.

Praise Him Right Where You Are!
Thaddeus Miles Photography

Day 8

Be Thankful

8 Finally, brethren, whatever things are true, whatever things are noble, whatever things are just, whatever things are pure, whatever things are lovely, whatever things are of good report, if there is any virtue and if there is anything praiseworthy--meditate on these things.

Philippians 4:8

Last night as I prepared for bed, I begin to think about what He wanted me to write for today's devotion. And it came to me. Normally, when I write these, it is passive for you; in other words, you just read it. But, today, I would like for this to be interactive. Many times we are so busy asking and requesting things of God, when the truth is, we really have much for which to be thankful. Today, reflect on some of the things that make you grateful to God. Post things on social media that make you thankful. It doesn't have to be something huge, just something simple. You can post more than one thing, if you'd like. Let's help encourage one another today.

I'll go first—I am thankful for peace of mind! So many people are troubled, but I am grateful that I am at peace with life as I watch it all unfold in God's timing and will.   If you are not on social media, you can write it here.

_____

_____

_____

_____

_____

_____

Day 9

How are your Management Skills?

21 For He made Him who knew no sin to be sin for us, that we might become the righteousness of God in Him.
2 Cor. 5:21

At times, we can falsely assume ownership of the gifts God has given us to manage on His behalf. Think about the whole reason He gives us these gifts; to be useful for His kingdom. We forget so easily that we are called to serve, to give of ourselves, to pour out, into others. We are called to empower others with more, to help them become better than they are now. That speaks volumes to me. I'm called to enrich the life of someone else! I'm called to invest into someone else's life! Christ did it for me, for us. His ultimate gift. His life, redeemed us so we could become the righteousness of God.

Think about this today. There is one major difference between The Dead Sea and The Sea of Galilee; they both are made of the same water from Mt. Hermon. However, the Sea of Galilee is vibrant and beautiful, giving life to the Jordan plains and other living creatures, while The Dead Sea is just that, dead. One has an outlet; it's giving; the other doesn't, it keeps. You are here to serve; that is your purpose. But in giving, it always comes back to you. When you don't, then you stop your flow of productivity and become as The Dead Sea. Thank God today for your ability to serve!

Day 10

What Do You Want?

1 A Psalm of David. The Lord is my shepherd;

I shall not want.
Psalm 23:1

Upon reflecting on this very familiar passage of scripture, the first verse says that I shall not want. I use to say to myself, "but there are things that I do want." Have you ever felt like that? But, in studying this scripture, it is translated to be, "I shall not want or lack any good thing."

Any shepherd is diligent in protecting, guiding, and providing for the flock. The shepherd does this with tender loving care. Likewise, the sheep know to follow the leading and guidance of the shepherd. The sheep trusts the shepherd for all of its needs, never questioning; just knowing that it will be okay under the shepherd's guidance. So, if He calls Himself our shepherd, then we can rest assured that He does just what a natural shepherd does. And we should do what a natural sheep does as well. just depend on the Shepherd. If we do this, then guess what? We will not lack any good thing! If we don't have it, then it probably is not good for us at that time!

We must trust Him to know, He knows what's best for His sheep! Today, reflect on the mere fact that God is aware of all our needs, wants, and desires. And He knows what truly is the best timing for us to receive. So, if we don't have it, then it isn't the right time! Trust His infinite wisdom for He really is God!

Tell God what you want.

_____
_____
_____
_____
_____
_____
_____

Day 11

Divinely Hidden Reasons

**27 John answered and said, "A man can receive nothing unless it has been given to him from heaven.
John 3:27**

Have you ever hated a certain job that you've held? I have. It was a call center for an insurance company. It paid well, and had excellent benefits, but I hated it. I took incoming calls all day for people calling about disability benefits. I always felt a bit of depression the night before as I prepared for work. I even hated the smell of the place, and I would get an attitude when I pulled up in the lot! In fact, my last day at work, before I moved back here, I went to lunch and just never went back!

What I realize now, that I didn't know then, is that God allows every experience to aid in our ultimate calling. Even if we hate the experience, there is something you can learn from it that will help supplement your knowledge for the future.

So, we can either hate it, become depressed about it, complain or accept it. Once you come to terms with it, smile, and learn everything you can out of it! There is a reason you're there. Oh, that insurance company that I hated....it has proven to have given me a wealth of information about insurance, about how to treat employees, so they feel appreciated, and the list goes on.

So today, be happy about every experience and use it. Replace your negative attitude and frown with a positive attitude and smile!

Day 12

Make Room for More

4 When He had stopped speaking, He said to Simon, "Launch out into the deep and let down your nets for a catch." 5 But Simon answered and said to Him, "Master, we have toiled all night and caught nothing; nevertheless at Your word I will let down the net."
Luke 5:4-5

Ever feel like as a Christian, you aren't blessed like you should be? Are we really prepared for more? Sure, we pray, but do we pray whole heartedly, believing it's going to happen? The Spirit of Excellences works hand in hand with preparation. When we believe God at His Word, we operate in the excellency of already having it; i.e., ownership. Don't wait for a better job to operate in excellency, but do your best in the position He has given; until He gives the promised job. In other words, act like you already have the dream job, house, etc. We have all heard the old adage, "God will never give us more than we are prepared to (handle) receive." Instead of looking at it in terms of heartache or hardship, ponder that question in light of this scripture; are you prepared to receive more?

Day 13

Make Room For More — Part 2

4 When He had stopped speaking, He said to Simon, "Launch out into the deep and let down your nets for a catch." 5 But Simon answered and said to Him, "Master, we have toiled all night and caught nothing; nevertheless at Your word I will let down the net."
Luke 5:4-5

Today, the Apostle is talking about keeping the family balanced. He said God, family, church, and everyone else, in that order of importance. He is also talking about love. The love we should have for everyone! If you ask ten different people his or her definition of love, you will probably get ten different answers. Many people associate love with a feeling, but it is not. Love goes beyond that. It shows, it does, it acts, it gives, it shares, it helps, it sacrifices. The bottom line? Love is an action word! And in ministry, we have to love! Ministry is about serving; it is service. We become too selfish in ministry. It should be beyond our needs, our feelings. So, as we make room for more, prepare yourself to be a giver. A giver of one's gifts, talents, and service to the building of His kingdom and do it with love!

Do you think people can miss his or her window of "more?" Do you think you've ever missed your window of "more?" God is too wise to waste His more (blessings) on those who aren't ready for it. Get prepared for more. Don't miss your opportunity to be a family changer, a world changer, a kingdom builder! Make room for your more.

— Day 14 —

What Constitutes Beauty/Satisfaction?

23 The fear of the Lord leads to life, And he who has it will abide in satisfaction; He will not be visited with evil.
Proverbs 19:23

Women are the most critical people. Not only are we critical of other women, we can be critical of ourselves as well. Don't get me wrong, some critique is necessary, but we tend to be overly critical of every aspect we perceive as a flaw. How many times have you looked in the mirror and said, "If I could just lose this excess right here, or have lighter color eyes, or lighter color skin? If I didn't have this type of hair?" How about this one, "if I had bigger _____?" Well, you get it. Men do the same things about their bodies, habits, and manly toys. Or have you ever replayed something over in your head and thought, "I should have said it this way or added that?"

If a child has gone astray, how many times have you thought, even if you didn't say it aloud, "Where did I go wrong?" There are many times that we don't feel as beautiful as we are because of this critical spirit. Real beauty is not about a finished or flawless product. Real beauty starts within and flows outward.

When we learn to embrace that God is the Master Artist and He is still working in and on us, then we will understand that the journey from brokenness to beautiful is a process. And whatever stage you are in now, you are still beautiful to God. For He knows and sees the completed work!

Proverbs 1:5   Thaddeus Miles Photography

Day 15

What Is A Family?

11 The heart of her husband safely trusts her; So he will have no lack of gain... 28 Her children rise up and call her blessed; Her husband also, and he praises her:
Proverbs 31:11, 28

The modern family looks much different than it did 30 years ago. Rarely does anyone have a traditional family anymore. Women of God, serve a purpose in the home. They are the ones who set the atmosphere. Whether running a single-family household or one with a blended family, they are to illustrate the love and nature of God when He created the family. God created the family before He created the church! That means that our family is the foundation of His love and therefore the first ministry! That means exemplifying His love through teaching the family all about Him, through His Word; but more importantly through actions. Depositing positive words and encouragement, spending quality time with them, teaching them tools to be successful in life are ways to show His love. Doing this will cause family to fully trust in you. Tomorrow, we will see the power words hold over your family.

Day 16

Sticks And Stones

3 Set a guard, O Lord, over my mouth; Keep watch over the door of my lips.
Psalm 141:3

"Sticks and stones may break my bones, but words will never hurt me." If that isn't the biggest lie, I don't know what is! It's right up there with Santa Claus and the Tooth Fairy. Words are very powerful, they can hurt, but they can heal too! Words are seeds—once planted, they grow. So, if you're planting negative words, it produces negativity while criticism produces discouragement; however, words of love produce kindness, words of encouragement produce hope.

Some researchers suggest that for every negative word, you need three to six positive words to replace the effect of the negative one. It's suggested that children perform better when this is utilized. They begin to think better of themselves. They believe they can really achieve it. I believe it works with all ages. Speak positive words to someone today. How hard is it to tell someone that you admire them, you appreciate their efforts or you like their outfit! The list goes on. Think how you can help someone feel by releasing and planting positive words into their lives! Keep your negative comments to yourself. After all, everyone has something that they do well; give them their "props."

Day 17

Unforgiveness

> 30 A sound heart is life to the body, But envy is
> rottenness to the bones.
> Proverbs 14:30

Such a small *typed* word, with detrimental consequences. If we allow unforgiveness to fester in our hearts, it continues to grow and retard our lives. It seeps into our gifts, talents, relationships, and careers. It alters and affects how we interact with coworkers, friends and family; even how we make new friends. Sure, we may be functioning, but deep inside, if we listen closely, our hearts are throbbing, aching from the pain. If we don't find a way to release it, we poison our lives and affect all around us. It's a root that lies deep below the surface of our smiles, clothes, makeup, hairdos, and exterior. And because it is deep within, most have a hard time identifying it. But it steals our energy, creativity, and our ability to reach our fullest potential.

Your challenge today, is to cut the root of unforgiveness and bitterness from past abuse, hurt, neglect, and press toward forgiving and being free! How? Forgiveness is a process. It takes time to slough away the layers of bitterness. Forgiveness is not overlooking or ignoring the wrongs, it is not excusing that person's behavior, and it doesn't minimize what has been done. Most importantly, forgiveness is not for the other person; it is for YOU! If you are serious about forgiving, then identify some areas of unforgiveness. Tap into the root and write down how you would like to see it change, so you can be free from the burden of holding it in your heart!

_____

_____

_____

_____

_____

_____

_____

⌒⌒ Day 18 ⌒⌒

Unforgiveness — Part 2

31 But those who wait on the Lord Shall renew their strength; They shall mount up with wings like eagles, They shall run and not be weary, They shall walk and not faint.

Isaiah 40:31

In the book, "Let it Go," by Bishop Jakes, He does an excellent job writing about how forgiveness is a life practice and it must be applied to every area of our lives. One of the things he mentions is that we must forgive the minor to protect the major. Your past life is too small to fit you as you grow into the fullness of what you are meant to be. Your garment of unforgiveness, is too small for where you are going. Since practice makes permanent, put into practice thinking beyond the smallness of the offense, to the bigness of where He is taking you.

Change your perspective. Change your height. Your ideas are a reflection of your height. Many of our answers are in higher places, far beyond the lower-level thinking. From a higher perspective, everything that is below you is small and insignificant. Be an eagle and soar! So, in order to become all He has designed you to be, let go of the minor, insignificant, unimportant, things of the past, and embrace the newness of your life! Get your life! It's waiting on you!

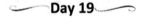 Day 19

Our Selfish Ways!

15 I will meditate on Your precepts, And contemplate Your ways. 16 I will delight myself in Your statutes; I will not forget Your word.
Psalm 119:15-16

Yesterday, my son wanted me to drop him off at school instead of riding with me to school and getting on the shuttle bus that takes kids of employees to his or her school. It required me to leave earlier than I would have to, to drop him off. Well, yesterday, just wasn't one of those early days. In fact, I usually have more of those days than earlier days.

He seemed to be a bit disappointed that I wasn't going to do it. I immediately reminded him of how he left something undone that I told him to do. I told him how that disappointed me. We did our morning prayer and I did in fact drop him off, because as a parent, you don't have to, but you enjoy doing things for your children.

In our prayer, I immediately thought about how we, as Christians, request many things of God and expect them, and we get disappointed if He doesn't answer the prayers the way we expect. But, how many times have we left things He told us to do, undone! How disappointed He is when we don't obey, but we have the nerve to feel some type of way, when He doesn't give us what we want?! Can you say selfish, self-centered? Lord, help us! Sacrifice your selfish ways, put them on the chopping block today.

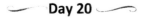 **Day 20**

Mental and Spiritual Health

6 Train a child in the way he should go, and when he is old he will not turn from it.
Proverbs 22:6

Having had the opportunity to observe students for years, it is clear that many have mental issues, anxieties, depressions, etc. Some have been on suicide watch, diagnosed with clinical depression, anxiety disorders and etc. Why do they have to experience such adult maladies at such a tender age? Where is all this coming from? Now, I know ultimately everything stems from satan; however, much of it comes from home life. When I meet some of the parents, I can quickly see why!

My essential question for my class, last week was: How are our personalities formed? Almost every student agreed that parents and guardians are the foundation of our personalities. Children read every page of the parent's life, good or bad! According to Sharon Jaynes, one of the *Girlfriends in God* authors, children find the methods of how to handle life through the parents. Not only that, they form their basis of who God is through the way we exemplify God! Parents are ambassadors for Christ, first in their homes before it spreads abroad! How do your children "read" God from your book?

Day 21

The Skinny On Fasting

6 Blessed are those who hunger and thirst for righteousness, For they shall be filled.
Matthew 5:6

Half the food we eat is not good for our bodies. Years of the American diet has produced both over-indulgence and undernourishment. Fasting is proven to rid your body of toxins and other poisons, while helping you not to over consume food. That's why you will sometimes feel sick while you're fasting. But, it also rids one's spiritual body of the over-consumption of religion and tradition. Fasting makes you more sensitive to hearing from Him. It's not another sermon, program, or conference that does it, although we like to think so.

Hungry people are desperate people. They will break past religious rules, regulations, and the norm for more of God. Only He can fulfill that hunger or thirst. When you hunger for more, you receive more. The Bible declares, as you draw nigh (close) to Him, He draws nigh to you. In fasting today, just rest assured that sacrificing that slice of cake (that no one brings to work until I'm on a fast! Lol), means I want God so much more than that cake. (Which by the way, has produced years of unwanted toxins and fat!). But more of God NEVER proves detrimental for my health!

— Day 22 —

The Skinny On Fasting — Part 2

6 Blessed are those who hunger and thirst for righteousness,
For they shall be filled.
Matthew 5:6

Do you understand how vital fasting is for every believer? Jesus fasted! He fasted to receive what He needed to walk out His public ministry. If He needed to fast, then how much more is our need? Fasting is not meant to be easy, because we are denying our flesh. But, Jesus knows exactly what we are going through. Reading Hebrews 4:15 lets us know we have a High Priest who understands, our weaknesses, but He conquered them all. So can we! God expects and moves when we add this to prayer and giving. If we understood this, we would fast more than required. Someone said, "You have to be serious when you approach God." Sacrifice seriously when fasting! Today, reflect on the importance of fasting, and approach it in a new and important perspective. It is life-changing! Matthew is about giving, praying, and fasting.

The wisdom of the world leaves us walking away from the principles of God. There used to be a slogan that said, "millions of people can't be wrong." So untrue! Because a majority of people are allowing it, doing it, saying it, doesn't make it right, or a Godly choice. We learn to be sensitive to His voice and His direction through praying and fasting and we must couple that with His Word. Fasting helps. When you seek Him, you find Him.

Whenever everyone else at work is eating that dessert or fried food, turn it down, for more of Him. He sees that and rewards us with more of Him. Be encouraged today, that your fasting and praying are not in vain!

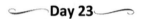Day 23

I Am Who God Says I Am!

> 11 For I know the thoughts that I think toward you,
> says the Lord, thoughts of peace and not of evil,
> to give you a future and a hope.
> Jeremiah 29:11

Last night, the Word gave me comfort, as only it can. The evangelist spoke, although it was just a mention, it blessed my life. We can get aggravated with life's nuisances and trials. If it isn't one thing, it's two! You know what we say. Know this, all aggravation is meant to stop progress; it's meant to slow us down. The enemy desires to make us expend unnecessary energy and attention to what is unimportant to reaching the goal of what God has called us to do and to be. We are not our situation and we are not even what others say about us. Declare today, regardless of all things around you, *I am who/what God says I am!* And don't stop your progression to becoming who you were destined to be!

Who are you?

_____
_____
_____
_____
_____
_____
_____

⌒Day 24⌒

Reason #199,999......

39 Therefore know this day, and consider it in your heart, that the Lord Himself is God in heaven above and on the earth beneath; there is no other.
Deuteronomy 4:39

Yesterday, while perusing a "to-do" list, I weighed my commitments and responsibilities against each other. I have motherly, job and career, church and ministry responsibilities. The list doesn't end. Of course, I grow weary at times, and many of these responsibilities conflict with each other. And sometimes—I drop the ball. I'm usually running behind time trying "to-do" it all. Which made me think of the omnipresence of God. He can be with me at the same time He is with you. He can handle my midnight tears with the comfort of the Holy Spirit, while He handles your midnight prayers. He can speak to my heart all the while, speaking to yours too. He doesn't grow weary, His times don't conflict, and He doesn't drop the ball. And He's never late, He is always right on time. To say He is God is so much more than I can comprehend. Whatever word you can think of to describe Him; He becomes bigger than that. Words are inadequate! That's the God I serve. I love Him more today! Reflect on the mere fact that God is with you, He hears you, and is concerned about the things that concern you! He can handle all of us!

⌒Day 25⌒

Busyness

13 but exhort one another daily, while it is called "Today," lest any of you be hardened

through the deceitfulness of sin.
Hebrews 3:13

Does anyone ever feel like they have way too many things to do? It seems to me that marking things off my list only illuminates more items that must be added. Even my mail seems to be too much to sort through. But, I believe busyness is a part of the enemy's tactic to keep us off course. The more we stay busy, the less time we have to focus on our main mission, and that is being ministers of this Gospel! Busy means...Bound Under Satan's Yoke!

How often do we pay attention to others around us? How often can we feel the needs of others? We stay so busy with our own needs, that we easily forget, someone has a much larger, immediate need. We are around people like that every day. Someone needs an encouraging word, a bill paid, a chore done, an errand handled. Jesus was busy too, but in the three years He walked this earth, He did more than most of us have done in a lifetime! He noticed others, His job was to serve, to fulfill the Will of His Father. It simply was not about Him and His needs.

We are here to serve. Today, admit you haven't been doing your job, and ask the Holy Spirit to help you to become the hands and feet of Him, to help out in any area. There is much to be done. Ask Him to help you become more sensitive to those that are in need; to help you see, hear, feel more of others' needs.

List the things God has told you to do that you have neglected to do.

_____

_____

_____

_____

_____

_____

_____

Day 26

God Sees The Best In Each of Us

22 Through the Lord's mercies we are not consumed, Because His compassions fail not. 23 They are new every morning; Great is Your faithfulness.
Lamentations 3:22-23

Doesn't it get under your skin when others just won't do right? Whether it is a relationship, friendship, family, church-member, co-worker or child. We see the wrong that has been done much easier than the good in that person. Be honest; we all do it! So glad God isn't like us! But, in that same person, there is some good, there is something beautiful, there is some wholesomeness, there is some righteousness. It's not all wrong. God sees the best in each of us. He looks past the failures, mess-ups, and wrongs, and sees what He designed. Everything He created, He called it good. He sees the good in each of us and because of that, He renews and extends His mercies daily! We must understand that for others and offer them the same mercies that God gives us. Learn to see past the thorns and see the beautiful rose. Today, see people from His perspective. Ask God to soften your heart toward His creation, so that you can exemplify His love to others. And that love is so deep, that He gave His son for us to have life everlasting! That's a whole lot of love! I admit, this can be challenging to do at times, but it is not impossible with His help and His love. Throughout this day, focus less on the negatives of others, but focus on the good qualities; just like you want others to do for you!

~~The Light In Us.~~ Thaddeus Miles Photography

~~Day 27~~

Communication

1 Now faith is the substance of things hoped for, the evidence of things not seen.
Hebrews 11:1

Communication is simply an exchange of information through a channel or medium, from a sender to a receiver. There are many things that occur within this process that may affect exactly what the receiver of the information actually receives. What the sender sends is not always received the exact way it was sent because of interference. It could be noise or disturbance, problems with the sender, problems with the receiver or problems with the medium. Our prayers are communication with God. It is not a one-way street and it is not mass communication, it's personal. God talks to us through His Word and we receive it.

We talk back to Him through our prayers. What's the channel? Faith! He can only communicate to us through the FAITH CHANNEL. Well, since there is no failure in God, that means the interference resides within us—our faith! Do you remember the older cordless phones? Remember how it would pick up distractions and noise, so you had to switch channels!? Well, sometimes, in our lives, we need to switch the channel, so we can get better reception! There is too much noise. We can't clearly hear His Word when there are too many people talking, too much gossip, too much TV, too much Facebook and other social media, and too little Word study, too little meditation, too little personal time with Him to distinctly learn His voice, and to build our faith. Too many other things drown out the Word that helps build us up in faith. It's not that God is not talking. It's simply we have too much noise in our lives to hear Him! So, the next time you pray and it seems unanswered, CHANGE THE CHANNEL, turn it to the FAITH channel!

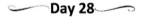 Day 28

Inheritance

> 22 A good man leaves an inheritance to his
> children's children...
> Proverbs 13:22

Christian parents are instructed to leave an inheritance for generations, not just their children. I believe this is speaking not just of financially, but also spiritually. It is the parent's duty to leave a positive mark on both. We, as parents, must be steadily preparing for our seed. That means that living from paycheck to paycheck, living under the burden of debt, is certainly not what

God intended if we are to leave an inheritance. That means we must find some vehicle of saving, investments, and the like, to do so. It isn't about waiting on some large windfall, it begins today. Start saving for your children! I was telling my son that saving money is not about how much you make, but about how you view and use the money you have. I told him about the story of a black woman who donated a million dollars to a black-historical college from her meager earnings as a "laundratier;" i.e., she took in clothes, washed, and ironed them for people. She didn't make six figures. But it was how she saved (or spent) what she had. My further instructions to him was that whatever he makes, he should live beneath his means.

Pay your bills. Teach your kids to do the same, not neglecting the principal of tithing. Therefore, the only inheritance we leave is one that has taught them how to live righteously. They will not have to avoid bill collectors, worry about cars being repossessed, credit scores being low, etc., you get the picture. We have a responsibility to our children not only to teach them about God, but to teach them about life. We have a responsibility to ourselves to also earn these principles and DO them!

BONUS
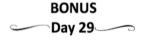
Day 29

A Family That Prays

28 Yet regard the prayer of Your servant and his supplication, O Lord my God, and listen to the cry and the prayer which Your servant is praying before You today.
1 Kings 8:28

A family that prays, not to be confused with the movie Tyler Perry wrote. Can you think of the impact that prayer can have in a family? We spend a whole lot of time going in various places, doing different things, working different hours. It's a bit challenging to choreograph our schedules, but it is vital that families find the time to communicate with each other and with God. Most of us have worship experiences on Sunday as our whole family is in the HOUSE. But, outside of Sunday, how much have we incorporated God into our daily lives, as a family? If the foundation of the church is family, then the foundation of the family is God. Let's make an effort to center our lives around Him, among our busy and hectic schedules, set a time to pray with, (not just for), our families! A song that I remember my dad used to sing, *Don't forget the family prayer. Jesus loves to meet you there. When you gather 'round the altar. Don't forget the family prayer.*

A family that prays together, really stays together!

Afterword

We pray that you have found this devotional edifying.

Should you find yourself in need of encouragement, this tome will always be available to you. Start from the beginning or earmark and reread your favorite passages.

It is a good idea from time to time, to peruse the notes that you have penned, as they will be a reminder or a gauge of the progress you have made. You can see the working of the Holy Spirit in your life and make a concerted effort not to make the same mistakes.

Contributor Biographies

Tamika and Mark J. Avery

Tamika Brown-Avery, a lifelong resident of Georgia, currently lives in LaGrange. She has always had two main motivations. One was to make a difference in someone else's life and the other was to become an author. She co-authored two books, "Faith: Through The Eyes Of Poets" and "Love: Through The Eyes Of Poets," with her husband in 2013 and 2015, respectively, with more in the works. As for the first ambition, she has truly been making a difference in people's lives since birth, but the most notable contribution was starting the non-profit organization, Youth Impact Unlimited, Inc. in 2015. Built around her children's vision of changing the world one youth at a time, its purpose is to share God's love, thus positively affecting the world through donations of time, energy, and provisions to those in need.

Mark J. Avery began harboring dreams of becoming a published author since the age of fourteen, but he lacked confidence and focus. Many years later, a young lady inspired and helped him find what he was missing (God and her). Mark shares many of his accomplishments with his wife, including those listed in her biography. They are also raising two children, running a youth ministry, and teaching classes on Christian marriage, but he also has a singular purpose. Teaching people about God is the most important thing in his life and writing is a tool he uses to serve that purpose.

Shayla Donaldson

Shayla Donaldson is a wife, mother and minister. She has a passion for ministry and a love for sharing God's Word with His people. Her desire is to encourage others to live the best life that God has intended but above all, her desire is to live a life pleasing to Him! She enjoys sharing her devotionals on social media and in other ministry forums, as God presents the opportunities. This is her first published work and she is humbly excited about how God is using her to spread His message across many different platforms.

Carla Gaskins

Minister Carla was, born in Savannah, Georgia. She is married to Shawn Gaskins and they have four children.

Carla is the founder of Tamar's Heart Ministries. Her passion to take God's Word to a hurting and lost world has resulted in a ministry that has reached thousands, through teachings and intercessory prayer. Tamar's Heart is recognized both locally and nationally. In the spring of 2003 Carla accepted her call, while preaching her first message in a shelter to a group of battered women and children. Under the anointing of God, she witnessed the breakthrough women received. That gave her a deeper passion toward women who were rejected, wounded and forgotten.

She has a passion, to see God's people living out their creative purpose and living a winning lifestyle. They leave feeling empowered, encouraged and uplifted. She attended City of Hope Bible Institute in Norcross, Georgia and sits under the teaching of Pastor Vincent and Felecia Campbell, at The Faith Center. She also trained under the mentorship of Prophetess Juanita Bynum at Global Destiny church.

She is the founder and owner of Life and Vision Connect and a certified holistic life coach; offering workshops and one on one life coaching for startup businesses and ministries. She is a contributing author to the forthcoming, *The Female Architect Rebuilding Your Life*. Minister Carla's faithfulness to build into God's people, PURPOSE, POWER, and PRAISE will continue yielding great results in the Kingdom of God.

Adrienne Goodlow

Adrienne M. Lewis, is a newly licensed Minister with Cathedral International Non-denominational church in Kennesaw, Georgia. Her newlywed husband, Tomie Lewis Jr, has been a great inspiration. She loves to paint with acrylics, often experimenting with textures, work with her hands and create jewelry. Soon she will realize her dream to publish her short stories, poetry and children's stories. Currently she is a Psychology student and her goal is to help young people discover the purpose of their art and use it to Honor GOD. She started a painting ministry and it has been a blessing to work with young talented artists and to provide encouragement and information for them to pursue their dreams. Her prayer is to bring these sessions to various churches to help the next generation see the beauty of GOD, express themselves and to produce artwork that will provoke others to want to experience the gospel.

If you want your prayers heard, become a worshipper.
—Mark Condon

Venus Griffin

From the genesis, the favor, seal and blessing of God upon Lady Venus has been evident. She graduated class Salutatorian, then went on to attend Georgia Southern University and is currently enrolled at Western Governors University, studying Human Resource Management.

Lady Venus surrendered to the authority of Christ at the tender age of 13. In 2009 she accepted her call to the work of ministry and was licensed as an Evangelist under the leadership of Apostle Cheristerlyn Brooks, of Holy Ground Tabernacle Deliverance Ministries in Statesboro, Georgia.

In 2010 Lady Griffin married the love of her life, Bishop Timothy Wayne Griffin, II. He served as Senior Pastor at the City of Victory, Inc. in Sylvania, GA. There that Lady Venus gave birth to a vision to reach and mentor young ladies, from different social and economic backgrounds. In 2012 she founded the AudaCity Mentoring Group, for girls and young ladies ages 5-21. The purpose of this group is to prepare and set a solid foundation for the "future" women's ministry of the body of Christ, by instilling biblical values, and imparting wisdom, with the motto *Defy the Odds, Break the Cycles*.

In March of 2015, by the leading of the Lord and the guidance of Apostle Allen H. Simmons, the presiding prelate of the Sounds of Praise Pentecostal Fellowship, Bishop Timothy and Lady Venus Griffin were assigned to pastor the founding church of the Sounds of Praise, Saint Paul, in Newark, New Jersey. Currently, the AudaCity Mentoring Group is planning to expand to Newark; where the need for this ministry is expressly evident.

"Lady V," is sincere and passionate about the work of the Lord; she is a lady of grace, wisdom, charm, excellence and power.

Melvina
Pratt-Harris

Melvina is a Christian Business Owner. She is married to Joseph and has wonderful kids, Tracy (Deceased), Tarek, and Mani. Her hobbies include sewing, journaling, and Crafting. She has a background in business, nursing, massage therapy, being a nail tech, and as a child care provider.

Stacie Harris

Stacie J. Whitaker-Harris is a Minister of the Gospel, an Author, Poet, Vocalist and Inspirationalist. She is an Advocate for Social Equality; holding a BA in Nonprofit Management from the University of Baltimore and is pursuing a MA in Law at Regent University.

Stacie is the author of *Hell and Heaven at 8,* co-author of the *Whitaker Book of Poetry,* contributing author of *My Now for the College Grad,* prior freelance writer for the *Baltimore Examiners Faith and Culture* column and visionary for the *Embracing Me* blog, reaching over 60 countries.

Whitaker's deep compassion, great faith, and resiliency allows her to overcome challenges. She is the loving mother of three Jewels who believes in fortifying the family.

I CAN DO ALL THINGS THROUGH *Christ* WHO STRENGTHENS ME

Bernice Loman

Bernice Loman is a global evangelist, wife, entrepreneur, CEO of Loman Creative Services, youth mentor, national recording artist, and musician. She has a heart and passion for ministry and seeks creative ways to encourage the Body

Teresa McKellar

Teresa is married to the world's best and most incomparable husband, Walter McKellar. She is a mother to three beautiful girls and countless others who have "adopted" her. She is a grandmother to three irrepressible grandbabies. She loves to read and write, but understands that her purpose here in this earth realm is to function as a prayer warrior.

Consequently, she is a bastion at her workplace and her workmates know that she will lift them up in prayer. Her favorite quote is: *I am just a nobody trying to spread the Gospel!*

Thaddeus Miles

Mr. Miles has a longstanding commitment to empowering people with a dedicated focus on strengthening the voices and visions of our young people. He garnered insights and strategies from his international work at Harvard Law School and Community/Urban planning programs at the MIT. This journey has reinforced his steadfast commitment to ensuring that the most under-served members of Boston have access to the same accoutrements of life as others.

He is the Director Of Public Safety at MassHousing and has founded or co-founded over five entities: Hood Fit, Think Big. Dream Big, VIP Collaborative, Neighborhood Networks National Consortium, and Mass IMPACT.

Nicole Peeples

Elder Nicole Bland-Peeples, youngest daughter of The Late Bishop and 1st Lady John Bland, has over 30 plus years of ministry experience. As a preacher's kid, she had very little choice in the anointed mantle placed on her life. Nicole was extremely premature and suffered many health problems. Early on, the doctors had given up hope but her dad knew the Great Physician and decided to dedicate her back to God. He had a reassurance that God would perform the miracle; He certainly did in 1973.

She currently serves as the Pastor of The City of Victory, Sounds of Praise Pentecostal Fellowship Ministries, Inc. She also serves as the National Directress of the Youth Department and sits on the Educational Leadership Committee, for the Sounds of Praise. She is author of the book entitled, *Who Are You Sleeping With?* and the founder of Designer Labeled Ministry, geared toward the encouragement of women, while assisting them in recognizing their healing, purpose, and power. She is currently writing her second book and first novel under the pseudonym, Lady D.

On a personal note, she is the mother of two blessings, Erik and Amariah. She obtained her BA degree from The

University of South Carolina in Speech Communications and her MA degree from Argosy University in Educational Leadership. She currently teaches eighth grade English/ Language Arts and was awarded Teacher of the Year for 2010-2011. It was an honor for her to be selected to serve on Governor Nathan Deal's (Georgia) Teacher Advisory Board for the 2014-2015 term. She is also a licensed cosmetologist.

Nicole's passion is to influence the Kingdom of God through the impactful teaching of His Word. *(I Timothy 1:12)*

Cynthia Perkins

Lines On Paper ~ by Cynthia is inspiring the world to write, one beautifully designed piece of paper at a time. It is her goal to supply the world with writing paper that is unique, fun, innovative and imaginative. Should you desire to write a letter, a story, study or just "doodle" around on the lines of her paper, it will be a heavenly experience.

Phyllis Smart

Phyllis Smart is a Motivational Groundbreaker, building and Restoring Confidence, by helping individuals replace low self-esteem and negative thoughts with self-worth. She is mandated to teach women to love themselves without labels, and help many to shift mindsets. Her motto is *With Soul Empowerment comes Self Improvement*. Phyllis is the CEO/Founder of *Next Level Living* where her mission is to enhance the quality of life for all individuals. Phyllis has been an educator for over 13 years and has a master's degree in education. Phyllis is a licensed Elder and author of a New York Times nominated book, *The Journey of a Helpmeet*. She is also an entrepreneur with her own line called *Private Worship*. It features Bling Tees, lotions, soaps and Lingerie. She is a wife, the mother of 6 boys a nana of two grand babies; and she is a native of St. Helena, South Carolina.

Prayer is not asking. It is a longing of the soul. It is daily admission of one's weakness. It is better in prayer to have a heart without words than words without a heart.

(Mahatma Gandhi)

Tabitha Vinson

Tabitha Vinson, dubbed the Motivational Worshiper™ and Internal Wealth Mentor™, is the host to the award winning radio program PWICU and she recently launched a new Thursday evening podcast entitled *Motivational Worshiper Moments™,* which is designed to give snippets of wisdom and encouragement to women to help them through life's journey. She's the author of *Check Your Keys*, which is book one in the *Keys* series and is founder of Vinson Publishing.

As an artisan, her workshops, dance presentations, writings and plays offer an incomparable panoramic view into the spirit of authentic worship and spiritual surges.

Life IS FRAGILE HANDLE IT WITH *Prayer*

Ayani_Meli

Ayani_Meli is a Child of the Most High, Author, (moderately unconventional) Poet, Playwright, Griotte and CEO of Revolutionary Disciples Media, and mommy to the most anointed, precious and handsome child in the world.

After graduating from Davidson College with a degree in Theatre, she taught at an alternative school and helped to establish Neighborhood Networks Computer Centers in culturally diverse areas in Boston. Currently she is sitting on a couple of Gospel plays for future production.

Writing is her ministry and her very first novel is *"Love Doesn't Live Here Anymore,"* based loosely on her life. She started writing it about a year before her Dad made his transition. Amazingly the Holy Spirit allowed her to write the words that would help her grieve prior to his transition.

Her second publication is a two volume poetry walk down memory lane, *Images and Rhythms of Generations.*

There are also two series of books for disabled children that Father has given her. The first series is *God Says—God Says the Struggle is Over, God Says I've Changed Your DNA, God Says Spaghetti Is Not Just For Monsters,* and *God Says You*

Are A Snowflake. **The second series** *is The Adventures Of Jessie And The Crew.*

Prayerfully, her work conveys that no matter how hard we try, there is always an area that needs work. Little foxes have a tendency to slip in under the radar; for many of us, it is with our love walk. Examine yourself, examine your relationships and recognize where the problems reside. Find a way to make things right. Life is too limited to hold grudges and harbor hate. The spirit of offense is running rampant in our society. It is time to show more love.

About Thaddeus Miles' 365 Project

My photography is an intimate gesture of composition: an embrace between what the eyes can see and the visual/journey of imagination. Though I am the photographer, it is you, the viewer, who makes the choices on what to focus—what to exclude. You are eavesdropping on a conversation between me and my lens and finding your own way into the feel and meaning of the work.

Throughout my professional career I have come face to face with the injustices and deprivation that fuel violent crime with tragedy, hopelessness and despair. I believe that detachment and denial are not antidotes. I have a commitment to support citizens of our communities to develop their voices and create their own urban legacy: to tell their own truths – about faith, resilience and community. A critical component of my work is to provide the technology, cameras, instructors and training necessary to endow residents with a multi-media capacity to tell their own stories.

But this is not my only reality. I also embark on a personal journey through my photography to reveal a shared terrain of natural beauty. Photography allows me a vision beyond hopelessness and chaos. A door is closed. A flower is open. There is a path along the river. I invite you to bask in the shadows as well as the illumination. Their juxtaposition in my black and white photography does not exist in order to blur distinctions, but to draw attention to the very nature of things – where we might stand in our differences on common ground.

With an intimate gesture of my camera, I invite you to make my journey our own.

We must be of keen sight to disavow our detachments and grasp what is embedded beyond our line of vision. We raise a conch shell to our ear and hear the sirens, the gospel music, the gunshots, and the jump rope slapping the pavement. Like an ocean of storytellers, we sound the discordant jazz notes of our common legacy.

Directory

Tamika and Mark J. Avery

Tamika Brown-Avery
CEO Youth Impact Unlimited, Inc., and Motivational Speaker

Mark Avery
Youth Advocate

Social Media Links and Websites:
Facebook: www.facebook.com/tamika.brownavery
Facebook: www.facebook.com/mark.avery.16

Shayla Donaldson

Mother, Minister

Social Media Links and Websites:
Facebook: www.facebook.com/shaymo
Twitter: www.twitter.com/gods_gurl83
Instagram: www.instagram.com/gods_gurl83
Email: smosley01@gmail.com

Tamar's Heart Ministry

Women Who Worship

Carla Gaskins

Motivational/Inspirational speaker, Certified life Coach,
Minister and Conference Host, Author,
Mentor, Entrepreneur
CEO of Life and Vision Connect, LLC--Coaching Service

Social Media Links and Websites:
Website: www.tamarsheart.com
Website: www.womenwhoworshipthemovement.com
Facebook: www.facebook.com/carla.gaskins.5
Facebook: www.facebook.com/Tamars-Heart-LLC-
1476354509250601
Twitter: www.twitter.com/tamar_heart
Periscope: connect_1life
Email: tamarsheartforwomen@gmail.com

Adrienne Goodlow

Minister, Mother, Entrepreneur, Artist

Social Media Links and Websites:
Website: www.theenhancingtouch.weebly.com/
Facebook: www.facebook.com/adrienne.goodlow

Venus Griffin

First Lady, Entrepreneur, Mentor

Social Media Links and Websites:
Website: www.audacitymentorgroup.com
Facebook: www.facebook.com/audacitymentor
Twitter: www.twitter.com/audacitymentor

Melvina
Pratt-Harris

Personal Concierge/Lifestyle Management Support

Social Media Links and Websites:
Website: (Forthcoming)
www.pharrisvisionenterprises.com
Facebook: www.facebook.com/inyourtime
Facebook: www.facebook.com/knicknacks2014

Worry ends when FAITH IN GOD —*Begins*—

Embracing Me!

Stacie Harris

Author, Poet, Entrepreneur, Vocalist,
Inspirationalist and Advocate for Social Equality

Social Media Links and Websites:
Website: www.2embraceme.com
Facebook: www.facebook.com/StacieJHarris
Email: GodsGiftLLC@gmail.com

Bernice Loman

MBA; Business Owner, Mentor, Composer
...
Social Media Links and Websites:
Website: www.berniceloman.com
Company site: www.lomancreativeservices.com
Facebook: www.facebook.com/blessbernice
Twitter: blessbernice
Instagram: blessbernice

Thaddeus Miles

Director of Public Safety at MassHousing, Photographer, Entrepreneur, Visionary

Social Media Links and Websites:
Website: www.thaddeusmiles365.wordpress.com

Theresa McKellar

Mother, Mentor, Prayer-Warrior

Social Media Links and Websites:
Facebook: www.facebook.com/teresa.ellis.mckellar

Nicole Peeples

Mother, Pastor, Teacher, Author, Entrepreneur

Social Media Links and Websites:
Website: www.LadyD.net

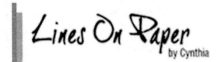

Cynthia Perkins

Mother, Visionary, Grief Counselor

Social Media Links and Websites:
Website: www.linesonpaperbycynthia.com

Phyllis Smart

Entrepreneur, Life Coach, Mentor,
Motivational Speaker, Authorprenur

Social Media Links and Websites:
Website: www.phyllissmart.com
Facebook: www.facebook.com/phyllis Jay
Twitter: www.twitter.com/DST1987
Periscope: DST1987
LinkedIn: Phyllis Smart
Books listed on: Amazon, Barnes and Noble, Nook Press

Tabitha Vinson

Entrepreneur, Radio host, Mentor

Social Media Links and Websites:
Website: www.tabithavinson.net
Publishing site: www.vinsonpublishing.net
Book site: www.checkyourkeys.com
Facebook: www.facebook.com/motivationalworshiper
Twitter: www.twitter.com/vinpub
Pinterest: www.pinterest.com/tabithavinson17

Ayani_Meli

Author, Poet, Playwright
Publisher, Mompreneur, Foster Parent

Social Media Links and Websites:
Website: www.ayanimeli.com
Website: www.jaribooks.com
Facebook: www.facebook.com/author.ayani.meli
Twitter: www.twitter.com/ayani_meli
Tumblr: www.ayani-meli.tumblr.com/
Blog: www.myinkwillnotstop.blogspot.com/
Publishing: (*Revolutionary Disciples
Media)* www.revolutionarydisicples.com

Additional Notes and Thoughts

_____
_____
_____
_____
_____
_____
_____
_____
_____
_____
_____
_____
_____
_____
_____
_____
_____
_____
_____
_____
_____
_____
_____
_____
_____
_____
_____
_____
_____

_____
_____
_____
_____
_____
_____
_____
_____
_____
_____
_____
_____
_____
_____
_____
_____
_____
_____
_____
_____
_____
_____
_____
_____
_____
_____
_____
_____
_____